Against Ambition

Against Ambition

Bill Peel

Published by Repeater Books

An imprint of Watkins Media Ltd

Unit 11 Shepperton House

89-93 Shepperton Road

London

N1 3DF

United Kingdom

www.repeaterbooks.com

A Repeater Books paperback original 2024

1

Distributed in the United States by Random House, Inc., New York.

ISBN: 9781915672032

Ebook ISBN: 9781915672650

The manufacturer's authorised representative in the EU for product safety is: eucomply OÜ - Pärnu mnt 139b-14, 11317 Tallinn, Estonia, hello@eucompliancepartner.com, www.eucompliancepartner.com

Printed and bound by CPI Group (UK) Ltd, Croydon, CR0 4YY

Contents

Preface

There's an old saying — a true one, I think — that every book is autobiographical. Every book is about the author and their concerns before it's about anything else. The same is true of this book. While it's got references to social critique, history, philosophy and literature, I can't ignore that a lot of it's about me.

I've never been a particularly ambitious person. For most of my life I never really wanted to make anything of myself or find a direction, to live up to my supposed potential. I made attempts, certainly, but they were motivated more by guilt than anything else. I applied for university out of high school not because I was desperate to find a career, or even because I was interested in exploring the field I'd enrolled in, but because it was something I felt I should've been doing, since I did well in school despite not trying very hard. If I went to university, my thinking went, I could tell people I was trying to make something of myself. I'd have something to tell extended family members when they asked what I was up to. It shouldn't surprise anyone that I decided to drop out in less than a week. I applied to university again a few years later and actually finished a course, but with my majors being literature and anthropology, few would argue that I was dead set on finding a career. It was more about doing something that I enjoyed than the returns it'd give me down the line.

I understand that my lack of ambition is an anomaly, and that criticising ambition is a tricky endeavour. When I told a friend about the idea behind this book, he seemed surprised, and jokingly said, "You're not going to make a lot of friends." Part of the reason for this is that when our ambitions bear fruit, *it feels good*. It feels good to succeed in one's work; it feels good to be recognised by one's boss; it feels good to expand a small business into something greater. If one has invested all their time and energy into their work, chances are that the few genuinely happy moments they have all hinge upon career success. But the lesson for us here should be obvious: just because something feels good to us on a phenomenological level doesn't mean it's always beneficial to us or the world around us. Things don't get off scot-free from analysis just because they make us feel good.

Marx writes in the first volume of *Capital* that "the consumption of food by a beast of burden does not become any less a necessary aspect of the production process because the beast enjoys what it eats."[1] In its original context the sentence is about how the things we consume — food, housing, tools, etc. — are necessarily intertwined with economic processes. Our enjoyment of something doesn't separate it from economic processes, nor from critique. A crucial part of any left-wing person's political awakening often involves coming to realise the cruelty necessary to create many of the things they enjoy, whether it's underpaying musicians to maintain Spotify's profits or rare-earth mining in central Africa to create internet modems. If we want to really enjoy using Spotify, or the internet, we're encouraged to ignore these factors. Ambition is much the same, in the sense that, because we enjoy it and its promises, it evades our criticism.

But ambition's value seemed to take a hit during Covid. Many came to feel they no longer enjoyed pursuing their ambitions, and lost their faith in the promises offered. Even though this book isn't a "Covid book", I couldn't help but be inspired by a brief interaction I had around March 2020, once the reality of Covid began to set in. The mass layoffs had begun in many sectors, and the requirements of my supermarket job increased dramatically as people began panic-buying shelf-stable essentials like dried pasta, toilet paper and baby formula. The supermarket I worked in had hired a fleet of short-term casual staff to meet the demand, and one of them was a very depressed looking man in his forties who'd held what he thought was a stable white-collar job until just days before. This guy wasn't like the rest of us at that supermarket: he wasn't a uni student, an immigrant or a dropout. He was a professional who had worked in an office in the centre of Melbourne, and who took his job and career very seriously. He was ambitious and, until he was sacked, motivated. None of that mattered when the time came for his bosses to sack him in what was, at that moment, probably a rational financial decision on their part.

Covid forced people to reckon with their ambitions in unexpected ways. Contrary to the logic of ambition, the pandemic showed people that their circumstances weren't always something they could control. In an article about losing her ambition during Covid, Amil Niazi writes that "there's an illusion with work that everything you give up now, all the stolen time commuting, working overtime, checking your email and Slack notifications after hours, will somehow earn you freedom and capital in your later years."[2] We're supposed to work hard now, save every penny, so eventually, when we retire at an increasingly old age, we can live the lives we've saved up for — let our ambitions run free, and invest all we can into them, so that we can reap the dividends decades from now. But for Niazi and the laid-off guy I worked with, nothing made the illusion of ambition clearer than the pandemic. Everything we've earned, saved and invested can all be taken away by circumstances far beyond our control.

Struggling to overcome one's circumstances is one of the chief characteristics of ambition. The idea that, if we try hard enough, we can rise above whatever conditions we were born into is an attractive one. One of the most salient definitions of ambition, from Alexis de Tocqueville, clearly expresses this characteristic. De Tocqueville called ambition "the desire to rise" and said that, owing to a successful revolution against the English, it was a specifically American affect.[3] When the Americans proved themselves able to throw off the yoke of English rule, and seemingly ordinary men became responsible for a radical change in their lives and their world, "nothing [seemed] impossible to anyone".[4] Ambition as I describe it in this book isn't uniquely American in the way de Tocqueville lays it out, but it's still seen as a desire to control one's circumstances, rather than being controlled by them. A recent self-help book for business types argues that ambition is a trait for those who "would like to have a say in where they end up", as opposed to those who are happy to let chance determine their circumstances.[5] Ambitious people are told, "If you try your hardest, you can achieve anything", and they actually believe it.

But there's another regard in which de Tocqueville's definition is wanting. What he didn't recognise is that ambition always, without fail, contains a sense of directionality; an ambition is an ambition *for something*. In the words of Chantal Jaquet, "The precondition for any ambition is the representation of a real or imaginary model that the individual desires to realize"; or in other words, to be ambitious is to have a goal set out in one's mind, and to do whatever possible to realise that goal.[6] Whether one's ambition is to be the best electrician in their small town, a world-changing scientist, or a leader of their country, one can't accurately be described as ambitious without having a goal in mind, no matter what it is. Even if one's ambition is for a broad abstraction, like money or power orrecognition, one has a goal in mind about how they'd like to get, and use, their money or power or recognition. De Tocqueville's definition is improved with this addendum: ambition isn't just a "desire to rise", but a desire to rise *somewhere*. When I write about giving up on ambition, I mean giving up on *both* these characteristics.

This is where the book starts. The first two chapters will explore how our desires for a life purpose and social mobility are not only flawed but actually encourage our willingness to be governed by external forces and ultimately to govern ourselves. The former chapter introduces Aristotle's notion of purpose, the "final cause", as an explanation for why things exist and its consequences for human life. The chapter argues that having a purpose in our lives is a source of unhappiness and restricts our autonomy, even if our supposed purpose is something we've decided for ourselves. Rather than giving us a reason to get out of bed in the morning, having a purpose leads to us to govern our own lives with a degree of discipline and micro-management that would be unacceptable for anyone else to impose, and for good reason. I argue that ambition giving our lives a purpose and a direction isn't a positive aspect at all, but one of its deficits.

The second chapter is about ambition and its unique relationship to capitalism, particularly when compared to other class systems like feudalism or slavery. What class you are affiliated with under capitalism is primarily based on wealth rather than bloodline or tradition; therefore, changing one's class is theoretically much more possible — and acceptable — in capitalist societies rather than in feudal or slave systems. People's ambitions can run wild in such a class system, because their upward social mobility won't disrupt the sanctity of the traditions upon which the class hierarchies are based. Ambition isn't only acceptable in capitalist economies, it's *encouraged*. Because if someone believes they'll ascend the class hierarchy if they work hard enough, they'll willingly dedicate their lives to hard work and self-sacrifice towards such a goal.

The next chapter looks at how people are made to be ambitious in the first place. Ambition hasn't always been as common as it is today, and from this we can infer that there are factors driving ambition today that didn't exist in the past. One of these is the rise of "human capital" as an economic concept, roughly the idea that everything about ourselves can be seen as something in which to invest and from which to extract profit. It's much easier to imagine propelling ourselves towards a future goal when we see the language(s) we speak, our social networks, and our interests as little more than investment strategies directed towards this imagined future. Ambition is also presented as a means to escape living situations in which we can't afford food or a roof over our heads. People like Andrew Tate or Elon Musk or Hillary Clinton, who can afford whatever food or housing they want and who are recognised for their personalities and uniqueness rather than being unrecognised workers like the rest of us, are presented to us as role models whose lives we're supposed to aspire to emulate.

The subsequent two chapters are about the consequences of ambition, personally and politically. Desires for social mobility and purpose introduce the possibility of failure into human life, and that failure can become a source of psychological dis-investment. Chapter Three is about failure as the inevitable outcome ambition, and how rare it is to actually get what we want. And since even those whose ambitions pay off are still compelled by economic forces. Their lifelong struggle to achieve their goals often only ends in disatisfaction nonetheless. Chapter 4 deals with the consequences of widespread failure and explores a theory of politics and power informed by failure and dis-investment in society. This is a politics of *destituent* power, which is characterised by the destruction and abandonment of a social order, rather than a *constituent* power, which takes the levers of power and uses them to build a future society. In this chapter, I tackle the paradox, at least as old as Montaigne, that the abolition of ambition is itself an ambitious task, and look at how destituent power is uniquely uninterested in goals and a desire to rise.

The final two chapters of the book are about what might happen — first to our relationship with work and value and second to our lives — if ambition no longer played a part in how we live. Chapter 5 begins by considering the various reasong why women are often considered to be less ambitious than men, and takes up the radical ecofeminist argument that women's lack of ambition isn't a problem with them and that the problem actually resides with men and the forces driving them to find their self-worth in producing things imbued with economic value. Women's position in the gendered division of labour — I argue, alongside the ecofeminists — is much better for maintaining the world and our ability to live in it. The work traditionally done by women should be valorised over more "productive" labour, and it should be shared by everybody rather than used to keep women in an economically subordinate position to men.

The last chapter describes how our individual lives would change if we weren't ambitious. I begin the chapter with a description of aimlessness not as a defect of someone's personality but as a positive characteristic. Some of the most valuable work has no broader goal besides the maintenance and reproduction of everyday life. Contrary to ambition's purposefulness, this isn't a direction in which to take one's life, but a daily practice of maintenance. I then draw on the French philosopher Georges Bataille and his work on wasteful — that is *useless* — consumption to show that the things we enjoy most are often the least economically useful, and thus the most wasteful. Bottles of wine, days spent on the beach, hiking mountains, hours spent gaming and/or chatting with friends: when we do these things, we're literally wasting our time on earth, and we're all the better for it.

1. The Tyranny of Purpose

All I am is what I'm goin' after.
                                    — Vincent Hanna, *Heat*

Government is the right disposition of things, arranged so as to lead to a convenient end.
                    — Guillaume de La Perrière, *Le Miroir Politique*[1]

Ambition is nothing without a sense of direction. For someone to be considered ambitious, they need to have given themselves a clear target, an aim, a goal or a purpose. The ambition to be a scientist or a small-business owner is commonly perceived to be good, associated with hard work and dedication to one's task, while the ambition to be a politician or simply to become rich and powerful is commonly perceived to be bad, associated with greed and moral corruption.

We see this distinction between good and bad ambitions play out regularly in films. Two recent films which make for an apt comparison are Michael Bay's *Pain & Gain* and Jon Favreau's *Chef*. *Pain & Gain* features three muscle-bound villains high on a diet of self-improvement seminars, ambitious ideology and protein shakes. Enamoured with the idea they deserve to be among the uber-rich, they kidnap and torture a wealthy man who goes to their gym until he signs over to them everything he owns. *Chef* shows a more positive, and modest, ambition. It begins with its protagonist, played by Favreau, working as a chef in a restaurant that's becoming stale and receiving bad reviews due to the owner's complacency and attachment to an outdated menu. A verbal confrontation with a critic leads to Favreau's character getting fired, and he sets out making Cuban sandwiches in a food truck. What makes the chef's particular ambition good, in the world of the film, is that he's not trying to become rich and famous like the gang of bodybuilders in *Pain & Gain*. Rather, his aim is like many of ours; he's trying to regain some autonomy and creative control at work. And by the end of the film, the chef achieves his goal. After his food truck becomes a hit, the food critic he sparred with offers to bankroll a new restaurant and gives him total freedom at work, similar to how artists hundreds of years ago would rely on the favour of wealthy patrons rather than government grants or the sale advertisements.

Just in these two films, we see how particular ambitions are assigned moral value based on what their goal is. Aiming for wealth and power is bad, and the ambition for them requires socially unacceptable means. On the other hand, aiming for autonomy and freedom in one's work is good, and can be done through "legitimate" means. But there's something we miss when we focus all our attention on the *particular* purpose ambition draws people towards. In saying that Favreau's chef lives for a good purpose while the bodybuilder gang live for a bad purpose, we're implying that the directionality and purposefulness their ambitions have given them is a value-neutral characteristic, not to be judged in its own right. I disagree. The problem I'm addressing in this chapter isn't which ambitions are good and which ones are bad based on where they are directed, but that ambition gives life an overwhelming sense of purpose and direction at all.

How could I possibly be against the idea of people having

a purpose in their lives? Why else should they get out of bed in the morning? Ambition is often defended on the grounds that the purpose people find for themselves gives them a motivation to keep living. But if we investigate the philosophy behind what it means to even have a purpose, we quickly see that any positive influence is outweighed by its negatives.

What was I made for?

To my mind, the first thinker one should consult on what it means for something to have a purpose is Aristotle, who wrote that "purpose" is one of the four causes, the reasons for things being the way they are. According to Aristotle, an act or object's "final cause" (or its "Telos" in Greek) is its aim, goal, end or purpose, and "each thing is defined by its end."[2] Insofar as humans make chairs to be sat on, if a chair is fit for this purpose, it's fulfilling its Telos. Similarly, the Telos of a gun is to be fired, because that's the reason it was made. Aristotle argued that the principle of things existing for a purpose can be expanded to include nature as well. Even though nature appears to work through random chance, that abnormalities seem rare was evidence enough to Aristotle that natural organisms work towards a purpose. That "all natural things are either constant or normal" was evidence enough to Aristotle that natural organisms work towards a purpose.[3]

We often explain natural phenomena in this teleological way, whether we know it or not. When children ask why the natural world is the way it is, teleological answers come to mind fairly quickly. Children might ask why echidnas, porcupines and hedgehogs have spikes on their backs, and we might reply that the spikes are there to fend off predators. When asked why giraffes have such long necks, or what apple seeds are for, we could say that giraffes' long necks are to reach tall trees, and that apple seeds are for eventually growing into apple trees. All of these are teleological explanations. We're saying that the existence of echidnas' spikes, giraffes' necks and apple seeds can be explained by their function in the present and future, not in their evolutionary past.

Here we begin to see why teleological thinking has received a bad rap since the days of Aristotle. In the current, more materialist age, it's preferable to describe the conditions which caused things' emergence rather than try to explain a thing by aligning it with a purpose in the future. To say that "giraffes have long necks so that they can eat from tall trees" implies they were *designed* for that purpose, and to say something is designed also implies a designer capable of creating a giraffe. It starts to sound very similar to the attempts to prove God's existence by observing bananas and how well suited they are for human consumption. Both rest on teleological assertions. These teleological explanations might have served people well if they wanted to confirm the existence of God as an intelligent designer of the universe, but in secular societies they're insufficient. A non-teleological explanation of giraffes' necks, and one favoured by contemporary biologists, might be something like this: "Giraffes have long necks due to a series of genetic mutations whereby the giraffes with long necks lived long enough to reproduce and the giraffes with short necks didn't." The non-teleological answer doesn't lead to the most vivifying writing, and will probably upset some children looking for a simpler answer, but it's the kind of explanation scientists prefer.

It's no wonder that Lucretius, one of the ancient world's most ardent atheists, was one of the few thinkers of his age to present a rebuttal to teleological thinking:

Don't imagine that the bright lights of our eyes
Were purpose-made so we could look ahead, or that our
  thighs
And calves were hinged together at the joints and set on
  feet
So we could walk with lengthy stride
[...]
For nothing is born just so that we can use it — in due
  course
That which is born creates its *own use*.[4]

Here Lucretius sounds closer to a contemporary scientist than an Ancient Roman philosopher, arguing that if God isn't responsible for creating things on earth, then things don't come with a built-in purpose. God didn't design us to have eyes so that we could see or legs so that we could walk; our evolutionary development led to our being able to see with our eyes and walk with our legs. If the organs came before their function, it can't be true that they developed with a purpose in mind.

Observers of social phenomena would also do well to abandon teleological explanations and focus on the causes of things rather than their supposed purpose. In the middle of 2020, when large riots and protests were overtaking many cities in the US, political commentators, particularly those on the right, criticised the riots because as an ineffective way of achieving the goals of racial justice. This is yet another occasion where thinking through an issue non-teleologically is more useful than trying to plaster a final cause onto it. When confronted with the question of why riots occur, the right can only answer through teleological references to their purpose: riots happen to destroy cities, to achieve political goals, as an excuse to loot shops, blah blah blah. When we eliminate the need to find a teleological explanation, we might instead understand riots in the same way we understand chemical reactions. Riots happen in response to an unacceptable event amongst a background of increased social, political and economic immiseration. This, I find, is an answer far truer to life than anything offered by the political right, and places riots in a social context that allows them to be compared to similar historical uprisings, like the German Peasants' War or the Arab Spring.

"But surely *some* things are made with a purpose?" you might reply. And yes, I'll accept that when people make things, like factories or bricks or pyramids, they make them with a purpose in mind. Marx famously argued that "what distinguishes the worst architect from the best of bees is that the architect builds the cell in his mind before he constructs it in wax".[5] What separates humans from nature, in other words, is that when humans work, they make things with a purpose in mind. But that doesn't mean those things will always adhere to the purpose for which they're made. Factories made to streamline car manufacturing can be turned into rave venues, and pyramids made to house dead pharaohs can be turned into tourist attractions. Closer to home, I find my dog Mango to be a particularly good example.

Mango is part Great Dane, part Mastiff and part a bunch of other breeds, all very large dogs. Great Danes and Mastiffs were intentionally bred as hunting dogs, helping people chase down bears and boars in Northern Europe. In a sense these breeds did actually begin with a purpose, but do the majority of Great Danes and Mastiffs today hunt large wild animals? Some of them do, but Mango certainly doesn't. In fact, ever since she was young, Mango has walked on her tiptoes, which causes her some physical discomfort if she runs around for long periods. So even if we wanted to train Mango to hunt, to supposedly fulfil her evolutionary purpose, she couldn't catch a wild boar to save her life. If I understood Mango through the lens of teleological thinking, I'd think she was nothing but a failure compared to all the fine hunting dogs that came before her — one of those things which Aristotle said exist "by the miscarriage of some principle".[6] He felt comfortable writing all these things off, like a rounding error, but I don't think of Mango as a rounding error nor as a failure. I think of her as the dog she is, regardless of whether she conforms to the purposes for which her antecedents were bred.

It's clear that teleological thinking — understanding the existence of things by their purpose rather than their cause — doesn't adequately explain why the world is the way it is. But the problem goes much deeper than that. If we see an apple seed as a potential apple tree, we might be scientifically inaccurate, but there's much more at stake when we try to view people's lives through their supposed "purpose".

Teleocracy: the tyranny of purpose

If self-help bloggers, management gurus, motivational speakers, hustle-culture entrepreneurs and pop psychologists are to be believed, finding one's purpose and working towards it should be the driving factor of our lives. A quick Google search for "finding purpose" shows myriad results, from all sorts of sources and disciplines, about why purpose is important for building careers, improving our mental health and basically everything else. Even though the Google search algorithm may prioritise recent results, I don't think the mass of writing about finding purpose from 2022 to 2023 is a coincidence. Covid led to people losing loved ones, careers and houses, and I wouldn't be surprised if, in its aftermath, people were looking to regain a sense of purpose as a source of stability and direction. But one's life having a purpose isn't an uncritical good. As we'll see, purpose and the search for it often become a form of self-restriction.

In the interest of full disclosure, I should admit that after struggling for a long time to find a halfway decent title for this chapter, I stumbled upon an interesting academic paper about Kazuo Ishiguro's novel *Never Let Me Go*, and re-used its title. The author, Tiffany Tsao, argues — I think convincingly — that the clones from whose perspective the novel is written are the best case to illustrate how having an all-defining purpose can actually be an oppressive feature of one's life rather than a solution to one's existential problems.[7] The novel features a group of human clones who have been designed for a single biotechnological purpose. They're a living organ bank, and grow up with the knowledge that over the course of their lives all their organs will be gradually removed from them and given to the "natural" humans, who are largely absent from the novel. The clones' lives will eventually end — literally described as "completing" in the world of the novel — when the last of their vital organs are removed. It's meant to be a sad moment when a woman at the boarding school the clones attend explains all this to them, but one could imagine her words said by one of those self-help motivational speakers who are a dime a dozen today: "You were brought into this world for a purpose, and your futures, all of them, have been decided [...] If you're to have decent lives, you have to know who you are and what lies ahead of you, every one of you."[8] It's easy to imagine a man speaking a little too loudly, wearing clothes a little too tight, running around a stage saying basically the same thing, preaching the values of "realising one's purpose" and finding what we're all here for. The clones in *Never Let Me Go* need no encouragement, of course. They know exactly what their purpose is, and they're taught it explicitly from a young age.

For a real-world example, nothing clarifies the role of purpose as an instrument of oppression better than the issue of women's rights. How would one answer the question of why women exist in the language of Aristotle's final cause? For what purpose can we say women exist? When put this way, the easiest reply is the typical conservative response of reducing women to their supposed function: women exist to take care of the home or to have children. This teleological justification for conservative gender roles became an immediate political concern for women in conservative-run states of the US when federal abortion protections were removed. In 2022, a ten-year-old girl in Ohio was raped and impregnated, and the state's then recent abortion ban meant she had to travel to Indiana to terminate the pregnancy. The case was brought up during hearings on Ohio's abortion laws, and the head of an anti-abortion group argued that "while a pregnancy might have been difficult on a ten-year-old body, *a woman's body is designed to carry life*", suggesting that carrying the pregnancy to term would've been fulfilling the ten-year-old girl's biological destiny, fulfilling her life's purpose.[9] As I hinted when I described my dog walking on her toes, and as I'll explain further in Chapter 4, evaluating anything relative to its supposed purpose introduces the possibility that it might fail. Not everything lives up to its purpose. If women aren't able to have children, or simply don't want to, does that mean they fail as, or are no longer, women? We see again how teleological thinking reproduces conservative talking points, and reduces women to their genitals and/or conservative social functions.[10]

Speaking of reducing women to their genitals, teleological justifications also invalidate trans women's experiences and struggles for gender affirmation. The claim that trans women are invalid because they aren't able to give birth is a common talking point among "feminist" and anti-feminist transphobes alike. There are uterus implant surgeries being developed for trans and cis women who want the capacity to birth children, of course, but I don't wish to imply these women are illegitimate unless they get expensive and difficult surgeries for the sake of desiring biological motherhood.[11]

One could argue that these purposes are only tyrannical because the people involved aren't able to find their own purpose for themselves. In *Never Let Me Go*, the clones' purpose is stamped upon them through strict socialisation and biotechnological engineering. Trapped by their socially produced desire to "complete" their lives, the characters aren't in control of their fate or their purpose. In the example of women in the US bearing the brunt of anti-abortion laws, their supposed "purpose" has been forced upon them through centuries of social and economic change. Like Ishiguro's clones, many women have come to internalise their supposed purpose such that they feel like failures if they aren't able to conceive a child. In neither of these cases do people adopt or pursue their purpose freely. As the instructor in *Never Let Me Go* says, the clones' lives have been decided for them. It's worth examining, then, situations in which people are free to find their own purpose, and if their purpose remains a source of domination once they find it.

One example is the titular character of *The Great Gatsby*. In the novel, Gatsby is well-regarded, as well as rich and powerful, but his life is miserable despite all his splendour because of his obsession with winning his old love, Daisy Buchanan. That Gatsby's purpose has dominated his life is revealed in one of the novel's most famous sections, wherein the narrator, Nick, recalls the origin of Jay Gatsby (quite literally, in that "Gatsby" is a character invented by James Gatz) and his love for Daisy: "He knew that when he kissed this girl, and forever wed his unutterable visions to her perishable breath, his mind would never romp again like the mind of God."[12] The phrase "mind of God" has drawn the most attention because it raises the question of what exactly the mind of God is; it seems to raise a theological question to which people get very attached. But I want to leave that aside and instead focus on the first half of that final clause: "his mind would never romp again". Where many authors might describe drifting and aimlessness in negative terms, Fitzgerald's narrator instead describes aimlessness as a positive, with the word "romp" highlighting the positive aspects of purposelessness. The verb "to romp" imbues directionlessness with a kind of childlike playfulness, rather than the more negative descriptions which could be used, like "shiftless". The narrator's description highlights the fact that Gatsby is *captivated* by Daisy in the very literal sense, that his love for her is holding him *captive*. Even though Gatsby can abandon his purpose at any moment, he feels he has no choice but to live his entire life with a singular purpose in mind: to one day convince Daisy to return to him, by any means necessary. Gatsby chooses his own actions and purpose, but Fitzgerald stresses that this purpose holds an immense power over him, and he is "forever wed" to accomplishing his goal. To borrow a term from the German philosopher Reiner Schürmann, Gatsby lives to serve a self-imposed "teleocracy" (coming from *telos*, meaning "purpose" and *kratia*, meaning "rule").[13] Even though it's his own purpose Gatsby pursues and he can choose to leave it at any time, it still has an incredible power over him and the course his life takes. To say he's "free" would be correct in a loose sense, but in a strange twist, his freedom to pursue his purpose becomes a source of his own constriction.

Gatsby demonstrates how teleocracy "forges a link between the ways we are governed by others and the ways we should govern ourselves".[14] If someone has supposedly found their life's purpose and seeks to actualise it, whatever purpose they've set for themselves necessitates a degree of calculation and self-management that borders on obsessive. We're given an example of this in a scene towards the end of *The Great Gatsby*, when Gatsby's father shows Nick a daily schedule Gatsby maintained as a young man, including a strict timetable and general points about avoiding time-wasting, saving money and not smoking.[15] Prisons keep prisoners' daily activities limited to strict timetables and we (rightly) see it as invasive and dictatorial, as we would if governments demanded the same thing of their citizens. But when he shows Gatsby's schedule to Nick, Gatsby's father is impressed by the strictness of his son's self-discipline and says it shows Gatsby was always going to be successful in some way. And it's true, his self-governance as a young man highlights how Gatsby has the right comportment to become successful. Always looking for ways to improve, to better his self-management, to maximise himself economically, Gatsby became an "enterprising self", "a self that calculates *about* itself and that acts *upon* itself in order to better itself".[16] This becomes necessary when one lives one's life in order to pursue their purpose.

This holds true for anyone who lives a life of ambition,

forever wed to a single purpose of their own choosing. Whether one's ambition is to be a scientist, an entrepreneur, an athlete, an artist, to set an obscure world record, or even as simple as raising a family by a certain age, working towards achieving these goals requires a degree of calculated self-management at odds with the idea of freedom and autonomy. Scientists need to dedicate years of work and study, much of it unpaid, to something they're unsure will even pay off; athletes are routinely awake to train at 5am; and small-business owners often work longer hours than full-time employees. They might be free from the constraints of having a boss and a nine-to-five job, but that freedom comes with constraints of its own: being your own boss requires making demands of yourself, and being available to work at any time ensures there's no separation between the time spent working and that spent not working. Moreover, self-imposed demands such as these come with questions we ask of ourselves that would be unacceptable if asked by a boss. "Is sleeping in an extra hour helping me achieve my goal?" "Do I have the time to have a few drinks after work?" "Can I continue to spend my time with this person, even if I know there's no long-term benefit from it?" It's acceptable to ask these questions of ourselves, because they demonstrate our freedom to govern ourselves, but in managing ourselves we are still, ultimately, being governed.

It's true that ambition gives us a sense of purpose, but if a life lived always with a purpose in mind is one of strict self-management, calculation and planning, we're wrong to suggest this is a *benefit* of ambition. Why would we want to free ourselves from the restrictions inherent to being governed only to then adopt a set of standards we can use to govern ourselves? Contrary to those who defend ambition on the grounds that it gives us a sense of purpose, ambition's purposefulness should be seen in a negative light, as getting us to make demands of ourselves we'd rightly refuse to accept if imposed by anyone else.

What a life without purpose might look like is a matter for a Chapter 7. For now, the more pressing matter is the defence of ambition as an engine for social mobility. Scrutinising this claim will be the focus of the next chapter.

2. Ambition and Capitalism

To believe that ambition is at the root of non-reproduction is to confuse an effect with a cause. If ambition is ambition for something, this something has to have emerged to make it possible.

— Chantal Jaquet, *Transclasses: A Theory of Social Non-reproduction*[1]

Capitalism is obliged to construct and impose models of desire; and its survival depends on its success in bringing about the internalization of these models by the masses it exploits.

— Félix Guattari, "Everybody Wants to be a Fascist"[2]

In every single human society, there have always been people who don't have to work to get the things they need to live: shelter, food, whatever else is required based on their society. In slave and feudal societies, there existed classes of people who survived off the labour of others: slaveowners, kings, aristocrats of many sorts. Capitalism isn't particularly special in this regard. Capitalism's innovation is that, theoretically, ascending the ranks of society and becoming a person for whom work isn't a necessity has become a much simpler matter. This theoretical possibility, which has proven itself real in certain exceptional cases, is the basis upon which ambition rests, giving capital one more ideological weapon in the fight for its reproduction.

What's so special about capitalism?

Marx is quick to remind us that "capital did not invent surplus labour."[3] For millennia, societies have been able to produce more than is needed to feed and provide for their working populations. In cases of disability or old age this is undoubtedly a positive thing; it means that those unable to work don't starve. But our ability to produce a surplus of resources allows the possibility of a class of people who are able to exploitatively live off the labour of others, and another class who have to do the work for themselves *and* for those exploiting them.[4]

In hunter-gathering, slave and feudal societies, surplus labour — and the resources created by that labour — served "to reproduce the community, the codes, and the relations of subordination".[5] In other words, a given community would have enough resources to survive while maintaining the traditions which held it together. Feudal societies, for example, operated by always sending their resources one step upwards. The peasants produced their means of subsistence by working the land, and a certain fraction of what they made would be sent one step above them in the social hierarchy, to the lords and nobles on whose land they worked. The lords and nobles would themselves keep enough to live and send money up again to their monarchs, whose land the lords and nobles were renting at the monarchs' behest. If there was still more surplus after everyone had their fill, the monarchs could offer it to the gods, or could spend it on expanding an empire, or something along those lines. This system ensured that everyone was fed, and that everyone knew who their masters were.

In these non-capitalist societies, the social hierarchy would also be determined, at least in part, by traditions and codes that seemed separate from the economy. The will of God was perhaps the most common explanation for people's socio-politico-economic status. Thomas Aquinas wrote that "ambition denotes inordinate desire for honor" out of step with God's will, and is therefore "always a sin".[6] The emperor Charlemagne says more or less the same thing, imploring his subjects that they should "serve God faithfully in that order in which [they are] placed".[7] In the *Homily Against Disobedience and Willful Rebellion*, a central document in the Anglican church, the authors write of ambition in the most negative terms imaginable, stating that it's a force of desire undermining God's placement of people into their stations: "By ambition, I mean the unlawful and restless desire in men, to be of higher estate then God hath given or appointed unto them."[8] The supposed religiosity of the social hierarchy wasn't limited to Western Christian societies either. Chinese emperors of the Ming Dynasty proclaimed that they had the "Mandate of Heaven"; their legitimacy to rule was conferred upon them by divine forces. Lastly, the caste system in India is based primarily on the Hindu *Vedas*, and someone's lot in life — whether they were a warrior, a latrine cleaner, a priest or a labourer — was in some part determined by their caste position, an "essential" characteristic. It's worth mentioning, of course, that according to some scholars the caste system was much less concrete and systematised prior to English colonisation of the region, but caste divisions and the hierarchised discrimination which came with them predated the English nonetheless.[9] The societies described briefly here are vastly different, culturally and geographically, but the important similarity tying them together is that people's social position was determined, to some degree, by divine will, and changing one's position was no easy process.

These societies did have some measure of social mobility, though. The popular image of destitute villages where everyone remained precisely in the same social position for their entire lives is not quite accurate. A feudal peasant could pay to go to school, learn Latin and eventually become a member of the clergy. Another route out of peasant life was to migrate from one village to another. One could arrive at a new village or town and offer their services as a servant to a tradesman, with the goal to eventually become a tradesman themselves.[10] Another method of positive social mobility is what historians call "internal mobility"; "movement within the group one already belonged to".[11] For example, tradesmen in a low-prestige trade like butchery could pay to have their children put into a trade with a little more prestige, like goldsmithing. Slaves of the Roman Empire could eventually be freed from their subjugated positions, but this all depended upon the goodwill of their masters. Despite these examples, "for the overwhelming majority of the population, a radical change in status was indeed a rare occurrence."[12] The vast majority of the time, a peasant would be born to a peasant family, would raise a peasant family of their own, and would almost certainly die a peasant. The same went for a slave-owning families in slave societies, and for royal families in a feudal societies.

Unlike the *qualitative* stratifications of these non-capitalist societies, capitalist hierarchies are stratified *quantitatively*. In other words, feudal class distinctions were buttressed by the idea that the classes were made up of different kinds of people on a fundamental level who were put in their position by God, whereas capitalist class distinctions only indicate how much money one has, and where it's going.[13] One's position today depends on money, and getting more money will ensure one's ascension up the social ladder, at least to a point. This is what

Deleuze and Guattari mean when they write that "classes are orders, castes, and statuses that have been decoded".[14] In capitalist societies, people's socio-economic position isn't determined by tradition, order, code or caste. Whichever *class* people are in in capitalist societies depends entirely upon how much money they have and their relationship to the production process: whether they have to sell their labour power as a commodity on the market or whether they have the capital to buy labour power to produce and appropriate surplus-labour. Yes, there are matters of personal distinction, whether one prefers wine or beer, and European art films or comic book blockbusters, but one's attachment to supposedly "lower-class" tastes has little to no bearing on their position in capitalism's economic hierarchy.[15]

Even a quick glance at the background of someone like Mark Zuckerberg shows just how possible social mobility is under capitalism compared to the preceding systems. Zuckerberg's parents weren't struggling to put food on the table when he was a child — his mother was a psychiatrist and his father a dentist — but this is hardly the generational wealth of someone like Elon Musk, or a French aristocrat from the seventeenth century. The film *The Social Network*, based on the development of Facebook and Zuckerberg's rise to billionaire status, emphasises his status as a twenty-first-century member of the *nouveau riche*, wearing a hoodie and flip flops to court proceedings and dropping out of university to pursue his start-up dreams. The point of this is not to heap more praise upon Zuckerberg for his entrepreneurial spirit; there's more than enough of that already, and such odes to the upward mobility of entrepreneurs "serve as political showcases and alibis to reject collective demands and contain people's sense of injustice".[16] My purpose here is to show how, at the very least, an ascent like Zuckerberg's up the social ladder from middle class to *staggeringly wealthy* (without having to struggle against traditions, codes and the kind of class one is assigned at birth) is a theoretical possibility for all and a reality for at least one.

What does any of this have to do with ambition? The point is that capitalism is the only mode of production in history that not only allows but openly *encourages* a desire for social mobility, breaking the cycle of reproducing one's own position in the social order. Recall in my introduction how thinkers of the distant past referred to ambition and the ambitious. Despite these declarations, people could ascend up the ranks of feudal societies through marriage, joining the church or accruing property, but those options were limited, as they are in capitalist society, to a lucky few.[17] And the fact that doing so was criticised in no uncertain terms by church and state alike highlights the antipathy towards ambition in historical thought.

Ambition as ideology

Now that we've identified just why capitalism is the only social formation in which ambition can be considered a virtue, we have to answer a correlative question: What function does ambition have in reproducing the capitalist social order? I give two answers here, but the latter needs more explication than the former.

Firstly, ambition brackets off the possibility of changing the world in any significant way and promotes people working as individualised economic agents. Whereas radical politics has traditionally questioned why the economy works the way it does and how it could potentially be changed, ambition is founded upon one's competing against fellow members of the proletariat for a limited chance at social mobility. When he was running for prime minister of the UK, Jeremy Corbyn was savvy enough to recognise that the political consensus surrounding social mobility was that is had failed. With the aim of replacing social mobility with social justice, Corbyn said that "the idea of social mobility where you pluck somebody out of poverty and promote them into a private school education or promote them somewhere else doesn't actually help the majority."[18] Adherents of the discourse of social mobility is directly antagonistic to the idea of raising living standards across the board. Rather, it homes in on a few select people — those with ambition, with good grades and who know how to navigate Kafkaesque government programs — and raises them to the detriment of all others. The discourse of ambition and social mobility cannot imagine acting *on* the economy and altering it in any way, and can only promote acting *in* a "natural" and "unchangeable" capitalist system.

The second benefit to capital is that ambition, like many other ideological mechanisms, encourages people to work hard and convinces workers that working hard is in their best interests. As Althusser says, ideology is the force that makes people "go", but ideologies work in different ways, and have different effects, so drawing out ambition's most pernicious qualities requires placing ambition alongside other ideological mechanisms like religion, state worship, consumerism and escapism.[19]

Religion was one of the chief ideological mechanisms of pre-neoliberal capitalism. Christianity in particular, the dominant religion in those countries where capitalism had spread, drew the most attention from theorists of capitalism. Max Weber famously argued that the Protestantism of Northern Europe and the United States resonated with the ascetic work ethic inculcated by capitalism, and thus was relevant to capitalism's early development.[20] The Protestant spirit of self-sacrifice and dedication to one's earthly tasks could easily be hijacked by bosses who wanted their workers to have an unmatched dedication to their work. Marx's antipathy to religion is equally famous, even if he did give credit to religion for being "the heart in a heartless world and the soul of soulless conditions".[21] Nevertheless, Christianity's propensity to preach "the necessity of a ruling and an oppressed class" and to justify the oppression of the latter by the former as the will of God made it a clear enemy of Marx's.[22] Without catching ourselves in chicken-and-egg questions of capitalism's emergence or blaming people for their religious faith, we can nonetheless identify religion as a justification for work and the exploitation of one class by another, and thus as a crucial ideological component of early capitalism.[23]

But the obligation to work hard for some transcendent entity wasn't limited to capitalist states. In many ways, the Stakhanovite movement in the USSR mirrored Weber's Protestant ethic. The Stakhanovite movement was born from Alexey Stakhanov, a jackhammer operator who, during one six-hour shift, as the story goes, hewed more than one hundred tons of coal — fourteen times his quota. This kind of productivity was of great benefit to the fledgling Soviet economy, which at that point lacked the industrialisation of its capitalist competitors and whose workers were described as unproductive by both Lenin and the *New York Times*, who certainly didn't agree on much.[24] In 1935, Stalin spoke at the first conference of Stakhanovites at the Kremlin, praising the movement not only for increasing productivity but as an organisation of "new people, people of a special type".[25] With their new penchant for heightened productivity, Stalin argued, the Stakhanovites were laying the foundations for a higher stage of the Soviet economy, which would necessarily need to outpace their competitors, as the capitalist economy outpaced the prior feudalist one. The suggestion one gets from the story of the Stakhanovites is that they were working for a higher ideal than personal recognition and the increase of pay. They were praised by the higher echelons of the Soviet Union because their feverish pace was working for the benefit of the struggling socialist economy and the approval of the state. I don't want to draw too clear a line between Stakhanovism and the Protestant Ethic described by Weber, but it's nonetheless a fact that both encouraged a kind of worker asceticism towards the goal of pleasing an external entity.

The regime of consumer abundance in the latter half of the twentieth century encouraged asceticism at work, but offered workers and their families a decent time in their off hours.[26] Workers spending forty, fifty, sixty hours a week on a factory floor won't tolerate their conditions for long unless they feel as though their exploitation is worth it in some way, and consumption provides the kind of fleeting, momentary joy necessary to make one consent to one's exploitation. But over time consumption becomes ideological; it prioritises people's capacity to shop over the realities of the work underpinning that consumption. One example is how we experience the relatively recent ability to shop on weekends and public holidays. For workers, this means longer hours and more obligations to work at inopportune times; but for consumers, this means that if we want to pop out and buy one last thing, even if it's at 11pm on a Saturday, the shops will be open.[27] Current proclamations about "twenty-four-hour cities" are updates of this practice, as they always focus on the people bar-hopping at 3am or taking the tram home at 5am, but never the people serving drinks in those bars or operating those trams, and certainly not the outsourced and precarious workers cleaning those bars and trams as the sun comes up. As this ideology of consumption is naturalised and internalised, people come to understand themselves as consumers rather than workers, and the solution to our woes becomes not to challenge capitalism but to expand people's access to consumer goods. Because of this, consumerism has proven itself to be more durable than religion, as our access to cheap consumer goods rises alongside rates of exploitation, in a pattern that doesn't appear to be changing on a broad scale. Succinctly, "the ideology of consumerism increases workers' tolerance for exploitation", which becomes "the price to pay for gaining entry into the paradise of shopping".[28]

Escapist ambitions are yet another example of how a love of work manifests itself, and should be differentiated from how contemporary ambitions are understood. Your average ambitious worker seventy years ago looked very different to an ambitious worker today. Ambitious desire then was founded upon wanting to escape one's miserable conditions, often to escape the economy itself. For example, think of George Milton and Lennie Small in Steinbeck's *Of Mice and Men*. They survive through the great depression of the 1930s by moving from one shitty, miserable job to another, and persevere through keeping the dream of escape alive. The more eloquent George repeats a story to Lennie, over and over again, of the two men buying a farm together and living off the "fatta the lan'". Later, when the older farmhand Candy gets included in the story, he recounts exactly what kind of conditions he wants to escape: "I planted crops for damn near ever'body in this state, but they wasn't my crops, and when I harvested 'em, it wasn't none of my harvest."[29] Their ambition is to escape their position as workers in capitalism, to escape their own dispossession. Sure, when the group fantasise, they mention that they could sell some extra produce on the market, but this is a far cry from having to sell their labour to keep food on the table every night. George and Lennie's ideal relationship to the market is similar to that of feudal peasants: a genuinely voluntary one, where the market functions "more as an *opportunity* than as an *imperative*".[30]

We can see echoes of George and Lennie's escapist dreams reflected in the FIRE lifestyle that popped up in the 2010s, standing for "Financial Independence, Retire Early".[31] By living an ultra-frugal lifestyle and maximising their savings, those in the FIRE movement aim to escape the job market as early as possible and come away with what they call "fuck you money", meaning enough money to be able to say "fuck you" to anyone they want without facing any financial consequences.[32] Ultimately, the dream of the FIRE lifestyle is the dream of the lottery, cryptocurrency investing and paeans to the "four-hour workweek", and it's difficult not to at least understand where those of these potential escapees are coming from. They're hoping to escape a detestable market they want no part in. And frankly, dreams of apolitical, individualised escapism have proven time and time again more realistic than the collective dreams of challenging capitalism. Who hasn't fantasised about walking into their boss's office and telling them to go fuck themselves?

Ambition as we see it now is fundamentally different from all these examples. The current regime of ambition is the only example of a justification for work that comes entirely from within, resonating with Frédéric Lordon's idea that the neoliberal regime of desire seeks "to produce *intrinsic joyful affects*".[33] The Protestant ethic, Stakhanovism, escapism and consumerism all have origins outside the subject and the work they undertake: love for religion or one's government is a joyful affect, but it is directed towards an external entity; access to more consumer items is joyful as well, but it's also directed externally; and escaping one's dispossession is an external affect as well, and its origins are sad, rather than joyful, as *Of Mice and Men* shows us. Unlike George and Lennie's ambitions to escape capitalism and live self-sufficiently on a farm someplace, the ambitious workers we so often see in neoliberalism have no desire to *escape* the competitive market and labour; instead, the desire is to *dominate* the market, thereby reinforcing it.

One could argue that the idea of a career or personal goal attached to ambition is an external affect, rather than an internal one. But, in fact, we perceive the objects of our ambition as conclusions we came to ourselves and attach them to our internal sense of self-actualisation. If someone wants to be a tech entrepreneur, there'll likely be a constellation of things around them which encouraged them to follow that goal: impressed teachers at their schools; school administrations willing to put on classes in programming or IT; parents willing to sacrifice some pleasures for those of their child; likeminded people to study and collaborate with; a culture that encourages accomplishments in entrepreneurship and technology; cheap hardware and resources provided by unseen workers in the Global South; successful entrepreneurs the ambitious person wants to emulate them; and on and on it goes. But even though all these factors have a part to play in determining *why* someone might want to go on to be a tech entrepreneur, the person only perceives these factors in hindsight, once the ambition is already set in place and their desires have been given a tangible teleology.

Ultimately, ambition's insidiousness comes from the fact that it's a positive feeling which we perceive to be coming entirely from ourselves and our personal choices. When we follow our ambitions, we imagine ourselves to be acting freely in the economy. But as we'll see, no economic activity can be accurately described as "free", even if we realise the entrepreneurial dream of liberating ourselves from bosses.

Beyond the boss

One of neoliberalism's chief promises is a degree of freedom unseen in prior economic systems. With the retreat of hierarchical management, workers were imagined to be left free to pursue their ambitions as entrepreneurial *Übermenschen*. But freedom from one's boss isn't necessarily freedom from capital. In the first volume of his *History of Sexuality*, Michel Foucault implored us to think of power in a way that didn't depend upon a monarch or a dictator repressing people from on high. As long as we see power as a repressive legal instrument emanating from a sovereign, "we still have not cut off the head of the king".[34] We should extend Foucault's lesson and cut the head off the boss as well. We cannot properly grasp entrepreneurial capitalism and the reign of ambition unless we begin to think of capitalism's domination in ways that don't depend on bosses or managerial hierarchies.

The neoliberal retreat of the boss can be clarified by the changing meaning of the term *homo economicus*, "economic man". To nineteenth-century economists, *homo economicus* referred to two people in a voluntary and equal relationship of exchange: one person buys something from another, and both parties seek to maximise whatever benefit they receive. This includes the relationship between bosses and employees, where the former buys the labour power from the latter and seeks to maximise the return on investment. This is precisely why, when he wrote of how capitalism came to be the dominant economic system of the world, Adam Smith could only imagine it as a consequence of the supposedly natural inclination of humans to "barter, truck, and exchange". Marx and Smith were in agreement that *homo economicus* — humans as economic maximisers — was a real phenomenon, but Marx argued that it wasn't a natural phenomenon by any stretch, and that it was instead a result of the capitalist market and the reign of exchange value. He wrote in his notebooks that "it is impossible to find any trace of distinction" between the subjectivity of labour and that of the bourgeoisie.[35] On this, Smith and Marx are in agreement: capitalism turns everybody — bourgeoisie and proletariat, young and old, etc. — into little more than "exchangers", out only for their own economic gain.

The neoliberals of the twentieth century held onto the idea of *homo economicus*, but its meaning had changed substantially from the days of Smith and Marx. Rather than economic man as a creature of exchange, they took it to refer to one lone person as "an entrepreneur of himself, being for himself his own capital, being for himself his own producer, being for himself the source of his earnings".[36] Whereas the model of *homo economicus* as one of two agents in a process of exchange highlights the boss buying the labour power of an employee — tying the employees together as individuals in a collective position in relation to their boss — the neoliberal *homo economicus*, as an isolated entrepreneur, minimises the presence of the boss as a dominant figure, offering workers a patina of personal freedom detached from the managerial domination of the pre-neoliberal workplace. The theoretical retreat of the boss matched the trends occurring in management theories of the 1970s, as vertical hierarchies of workplace command were being replaced by more horizontal structures often compared to a network, wherein employees could almost be left alone so long as their goals matched those of the company.[37] These changes reinforced the idea that bosses had stopped mattering, and everyone was out for themselves as competing entrepreneurs.

Despite what its defenders might say, the emergence of neoliberalism and the retreat of hierarchical management was not the unleashing of an ultimate freedom. Rather, it can be better understood as the transition from one form of power to another. In his recent book *Mute Compulsion*, Søren Mau draws on Marx's famous line that once capitalism had been, "written in the annals of mankind in letters of blood and fire", it didn't need to rely entirely upon blood and fire — direct violent coercion — to reproduce itself.[38] Instead, capital could rely upon the "mute compulsion of economic relations" that the competitive market already put in place.[39] Marx's innovation, which Mau explicates in his book, is to have imagined a form of power distinct from coercion of the body or ideological affecting of the mind. Instead, this third form of power, "economic power", structures an environment and manages the possibilities within it, without even needing to act upon people specifically.[40] A basic example is when conservative commentators respond to complaints about expensive housing or shitty workplace conditions by arguing that "If you don't like it, leave!", obviously ignoring the fact that shelter and food are both human necessities which require money and, therefore, a job. Economic power structures people's environments the same way that gills structure the environment of fish: the fish understands innately that it needs to stay underwater to stay alive. The same is true of human life in any capitalist society: to reproduce ourselves day-to-day requires engaging with the market in some way, either to buy things to eat or to work to afford to live. This shows that the transition from social democracy to neoliberalism wasn't an absolute decrease of power. Instead, it was a transition from the coercive power of the state or the boss to the mute compulsion of economic power. What Milton Friedman called the "competitive order" of the free market came to power.[41]

Mistaking economic power for coercive power — the "mute compulsion" of the economy for the direct power of bosses or the state — can mistakenly promote the idea that being our own boss makes us free. Despite his astute descriptions of how we've come to enjoy work, this is a mistake Frédéric Lordon makes in his book *Willing Slaves of Capital*. Ironically, given the book's title, Lordon centres bosses as the chief masters of the economy, rather than capital itself. Lordon's analysis of the contest of desires between bosses and employees begins with the diagram below — which I've partly simplified — as a jumping-off point.

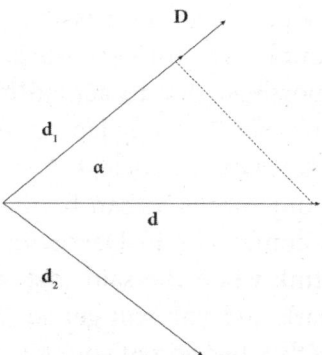

The diagram looks quite complicated at first glance, but it's actually pretty simple. The lowercase d's are the desires of the employees of a company, which can be pointed in three different directions: d_1 is the employees' desire that matches the desire of the boss, and which is thus maximally useful to the boss and the company in general; d is the employees' everyday desires, which drift away from the desires of bosses and companies; and d_2 is the employees' desire that outright refuses to be subordinated to that of the bosses, Lordon describes the politics that refuses work as a kind of "becoming-orthogonal", refusing the imposed usefulness of work.[42] The uppercase D is the desire of the bosses — Lordon calls it the "master-desire" — with the task of what Lordon calls "co-linearisation", the subordination of employees' desires to its overall goal: accumulating capital and delivering shareholder profit. The last remaining symbol, the cosine α, is the degree of drift of the employees' desires away from desires which can be instrumentalised by the boss. In a company, it's the boss's job to get as close to "α = 0" as possible, which would mean total subordination of employees' desire to the will of the boss, and thus to the company and its goals of capital accumulation. After all, when one gets paid, the boss has bought all of our *potential* work — our labour power — during a certain period of time, and the boss's goal is to actualise as much of that potential work as possible, turning labour power into labour. This might seem all very theoretical, but every now and then someone spells it out simple as can be. At the 2023 World Economic Forum conference in Davos, the CEO of Vimeo made a bit of a stink when she said that "it's not just your body, it's your heart; and you will get so much better work out of somebody if they feel part of your culture and mission." Obviously, the necessity for bosses to orient the desires of their employees has always been present in one way or another, but it's so rarely stated aloud that it came as a shock to people at the time, who were more used to online companies preaching about wellness.

Though Lordon is correct in his assessment that it's the job of the boss to subjugate the employees' desires to their own, by putting the emphasis on "the boss" rather than on capital itself, he misses that capital can subjugate desires which fall outside the direct boss–employee relationship. Let's say, for example, that a worker spends all day working in a "bullshit job" where little actual work needs to be done.[43] They sit at a desk, in front of a computer, doing a couple hours of work a day and filling in the rest of the day by pretending to look far busier than they actually are — following George Costanza's advice and walking around looking irritated. As far as Lordon is concerned, this constitutes a deviation from the master-desire of the boss, a refusal of the boss's co-linearisation. But what if, then, this worker with a bullshit job spends six hours a day doing one of many side hustles available to people online? Maybe they're doing freelance graphic design work; maybe they're completing online consumer surveys; maybe they're ghostwriting essays for high school and university students at hundreds of dollars a pop. What if they're not even doing a side hustle? What if they're wasting time the more common ways, watching YouTube videos or Netflix or porn, scrolling Twitter, TikTok, Instagram or anything else? Are these examples of freed, unsubordinated desire? If we centre *the boss* as the figure which subordinates desire, then our answer is yes, and these practices of side-hustling and consumption are a strike at the heart of the boss. But, if we centre capital itself, on a broader scale, the answer is of course no — individual entrepreneurship and consuming media products are still activities plugged into the capitalist market. Therefore, we should de-emphasise the way in which *bosses* direct our desires towards their ends and highlight the ways in which *capital itself*, and its economic power, directs our desires, whether in the workplace or out of it.

Part of the reason why neoliberalism is so insidious is because it tricks us into thinking that we are free just because our bosses no longer resemble slaveowners or the industrial capitalists of Victorian England. In a sense, Marx predicted this when he wrote that

> it is not individuals who are set free by free competition; it is, rather, capital which is set free [...] the movement of individuals within the pure conditions of capital appears as their freedom; which is then also again dogmatically propounded as such through constant reflection back on the barriers torn down by free competition.[44]

In the *laissez-faire* market so beloved by neoliberals like Milton Friedman, people are only free insofar as they're free to act within the limits set by capital, and the limited freedom capitalism provides looks all the sweeter when it's compared to slave societies either of the past or contemporary slave markets overseas.[45] This is a fact that hasn't changed since Marx's time. The retreat of the boss, and the turn from vertical workplace hierarchies to horizontal collaborative networks, appears to be one more step towards ultimate human freedom, one more obstacle removed in our path to greatness.

Conclusion

When it comes to ambition, the success of neoliberalism is in casting these very capitalistic ambitions as the *ne plus ultra* of human freedom. To ambitious people, Milton Friedman's "competitive order" is not something to be overcome or destroyed or even challenged but one more game to be won, and the process of winning is all the more possible once the typical representation of the boss has left the picture. If a person wants to be a finance exec, a pop star, a commercial landlord, a pilot, a mindfulness blogger or whatever else, the closer they get to accomplishing these goals, the more they are paralleled by feelings of personal freedom and self-actualisation. Ambitious people are constantly looking to improve themselves, and to seek new opportunities while making themselves more marketable in the process. They love doing so independently. They don't need to be told to act in a way that benefits the economy; they perceive their entrepreneurial self-maximisation as being in their best interests.[46] Moreover, casting the ruling class as simply more ambitious gives the impression that it's the personal choices and failures of the working class that put us in our unappealing position. As far as the discourse of ambition is concerned, there are ambitious people and there are the losers, slackers, vagabonds and louts getting in the way.

3. Producing Ambitious Subjects: or, How to Make Someone Want Something

Economics are the method; the object is to change the heart and soul.

— Margaret Thatcher[1]

Capitalism is [...] personified in the ideological figure of the tireless middle-class self-improver.
— Hadas Weiss, *We Have Never Been Middle Class*[2]

As we saw in the previous chapter, ambition can only blossom in capitalist societies, where social mobility is theoretically much more plausible. In turn, the possibility of social mobility serves a crucial ideological purpose in the reproduction of capitalism as the carrot on a stick dangled in front of workers. But there's more to it than that. Ambitious subjects — people who understand themselves and their place in the world through their ambition — need more than strictly economic motivations. But to properly understand that, we need to introduce what "the subject" means in philosophy.

Subjects and Subjectivities
Putting it simply, to be a certain kind of subject is to understand oneself and one's position in the world in a particular way that informs one's thoughts and actions. On

the occasions when someone is asked to describe or define themselves, they're implicitly being asked to outline the constellation of features that make up their subjectivity: what their socio-economic position is; whether they're white or a person of colour; whether they're a man, woman or non-binary person; what their job is; what their hobbies are; what their family background is/was like; and so on. A lower-middle-class white woman from the UK is going to have a completely different subjectivity from an upper-class Chinese man from Hong Kong, for example, because they've gone through very different processes of subjectivation. And there is a vast chasm between what is expected of these two people, and between what they expect of themselves.

As far as I'm concerned, the chief philosopher of subjectivity and subjectivation is Michel Foucault. Though his books *Discipline and Punish* and *The History of Sexuality* differ significantly, common in both is the idea that subjectivation is not merely a negating, dominating and repressive force. Contrary to the bad readings of Foucault that preoccupy themselves with the idea that people are made subjects through top-down, negative and authoritative measures, Foucault argues that we should evaluate the processes of subjectivation not by what they *prevent* from emerging, but from what they *encourage*.[3] Power works to "incite, reinforce, control, monitor, optimize, and organize the forces under it", and is "bent on generating forces, making them grow, and ordering them, rather than [...] impeding them, making them submit, or destroying them".[4]

To use a couple of examples near and dear to Foucault's heart, we'll look at how this dual notion of subjectivity — affirming some qualities and negating others — works in schools and workplaces. Schools don't only aim to curb the disruptive behaviours of "bad students", they also aim to produce the studious, self-disciplined and quiet behaviours of "good students". Managerial discipline in the workplace — which today looks more like deadlines and keystroke monitoring rather than direct oversight from a supervisor — doesn't only negate the inattentive and lazy behaviours of "bad workers", but also incentivises the behaviours of "good workers": willingness to work when off the clock, to work according to workplace guidelines, to report colleagues to managers, and more. Disciplinary practices seek to diminish people's capacity for disobedience while increasing their economic utility; it's not strictly a matter of one or the other.[5] Though Foucault's topic is different in his *History of Sexuality*, his insistence on the affirmative production of subjects, rather than their negative restriction, remains the same. When we think of Victorian England in the nineteenth century, we tend to think of it as a deeply repressive society in regard to sex. While there was no doubt some repression, Foucault insists that repression's negating force played a secondary role, and that an affirmative force was of primary importance: the production of certain kind of sexual subject. Confession was one of its most important measures, "a ritual discourse in which the speaking subject is also the subject of the statement".[6] The confessor is impelled to reveal themselves to a religious authority — thus producing and laying bare their subjectivity.

Foucault emphasises affirmative forces of subjectivation rather than negating ones, but it's often difficult to make a distinction between the two. Where do we draw the line between the practices that restrict bad students and those which produce good students? The mechanisms in place are often the exact same: strict teachers, identical uniforms, severe punishments from school administrators, and so on. Sometimes it risks being a distinction without a difference. Thankfully, the case of ambition makes Foucault's account of affirmative subjectivation much clearer.

For good reason, an ambitious subjectivity is rarely seen as the result of a negative and repressive force. The idea of someone being beaten until they become ambitious is ludicrous indeed. Rather, ambition is understood as the joyful releasing of one's fetters, an *abundance* of affirmation that overcomes any and all negating restrictions. I already showed in the last chapter how ambition often comes with the idea of fleeing the typical workplace and becoming one's own boss, casting off the restrictions of the nine-to-five job and becoming more "flexible" or "independent" in one's work. In how many stories does a character flee the stultifying atmosphere of their provincial hometown, seeking to make a name for themselves in a big city? The *Bildungsroman* genre is so chock-full of this type of story that it practically constitutes a sub-genre: noble, ambitious protagonists fleeing their reactionary families, their teachers who don't believe in them, their clique of friends with tall-poppy syndrome. These are so many negating forces to be thrown off on the protagonist's quest for self-realisation, self-actualisation and self-creation. We see here how ambitious subjectivity often becomes a quest to discover oneself.

We love to proclaim the benefits of self-realisation — "becoming who we are" in one of Nietzsche's most overused phrases — but embracing one's subjectivity comes with its downsides. A lot of French philosophy kicking around in the twentieth century stressed the ways in which subjectivity can become a gilded cage. In his essay "The Subject and Power", Foucault makes the point that "there are two meanings of the word 'subject': subject to someone else by control and dependence; and tied to his own identity by a conscience or self-knowledge."[7] The former can be found in phrases like "royal subjects" or "colonial subjects", and the latter in the idea of the subject fleshed out thus far. The resonance between these two meanings is why Foucault and his French contemporaries were usually sceptical of claims about a "revolutionary subject" in the Marxist tradition. In a secularising epoch without kings, there can be no such thing as a "religious subject" or a "royal subject", but there are subjects who are as tied to their self-identification as devoted royal subjects were to their monarchs.[8] If the way someone understands their life as meaningful is tied to society as it currently exists, it makes it very difficult for that person to be willing to change society, even if, intellectually, they recognise the need for certain changes to be made to how society functions.

We can find an obvious example of this in the politics of work. One of the perennial features of communist philosophy since the late twentieth century has been the struggle both against work *and* against the attachment to work inculcated by capitalist subjectivity.[9] The violence meted out to unruly peasants in the transition to capitalism affected those peasants' understanding of themselves. They not only became the *subjects* of capitalists, dependent on them for wages to buy the necessities of life that now had to be purchased at the market, but the legislation against them also worked to ensure they became subject to themselves as *workers*, distinct from peasants.[10] Turning peasants into willing and disciplined wage labourers took much more than expropriating their property. It took centuries of violent subjectivation, backed up by the legal system, to create a working class which looked at capitalism as a series of "self-evident natural laws".[11] The supposedly self-evident nature of capitalism has survived to this day, even if the precise subjectivity of contemporary workers has changed.

Human capital

In a recent book, the Marxist philosopher Jason Read writes that "the production of subjectivity does not end with the formation of a working class but continues and changes with each change of capitalism."[12] What this means in effect is that the subjectivity of workers in the nineteenth century, produced through centuries of violence, dispossession and compulsory work-discipline, is very different from the subjectivity of people today, as capitalism itself has changed.

One of the defining features of our neoliberal period is "the rise of human capital as a dominant subjective form".[13] Whereas the subject of liberal capitalism in the nineteenth century understood themselves as a worker who sells themselves and their time to a boss for a certain number of hours in a day, the neoliberal subject understands their lives as both a result and a process of strategic investments, and themselves as the manager of "a portfolio of conducts pertaining to all the aspects of their lives".[14] Originally, human capital referred to education and on-the-job training, and how these things could lead to economic benefits down the line, but the idea quickly snowballed to the point where one's human capital is indistinguishable from oneself.

> The things that I inherit, the things that happen to me, and the things I do all contribute to the maintenance or the deterioration of my human capital. More radically put, *my human capital is me*, as a set of skills and capabilities that is modified by all that affects me and all that I effect.[15]

The original conception of human capital can be thought of in terms of those hypothetical calculations we often make in our heads: "If I work after high school, I'll make a certain amount of money in a year, but there will be less career growth in the future; whereas if I go to university I'll be in debt, but I'll hopefully make much more money in the future." Now human capital involves not just the economic outcomes of education and workplace training but our predispositions to disease, our circle of friends, or tastes in media and art, our social and communication skills, our physical attractiveness in line with social mores, and so much else.

People don't just get tricked into thinking of themselves a certain way, and the same is true here. We came to understand ourselves as human capital due to material processes, just like any other form of subjectivity. Hadas Weiss suggests that the turn towards human capital is emblematic of a larger trend in neoliberal capitalism. Human capital becomes the focus of your investment when you either can't rely on the stability of economic investments or simply don't have enough economic capital to invest.[16] In an unstable real estate market, for example, potential investors might hesitate to buy properties for the sake of renting them out, since their returns are uncertain. That money might be better spent on their children's education, whereby they can be sent to fancy private schools, receive a better education than in poorly funded public schools and form social bonds with people of a better-off social class than those economically forced to attend public schools. On a smaller economic scale, and within the lifetime of a single person, consider the massive rise of self-directed online education in the past decade or so, offered through websites like Masterclass, Skillshare and YouTube.[17] People flocked to these sites during the height of Covid, of course; but before 2020, people seeking to educate themselves online were also responding to poor financial circumstances and repeated claims that millennials will never have a steady career. If university fees are rising, and won't even offer you a lifelong career in the way they used to, why would you bother? It's both cheaper and easier to learn through watching YouTube videos, and those who educate online claim that they possess the real skills necessary to get a job, rather than offer mere university credentialism. In short, "the more expensive and less rewarding material advantages become, the greater the emphasis on human capital".[18]

Since the value of human capital "is always only relative to what everyone else brings to the table", it encourages ruthless competition between individual people, who come to understand themselves as investors seeking to maximise their returns over others'.[19] Human capital inculcates an ethos of ambition as a competitive mechanism, as the unrelenting struggle upwards that characterises ambition is at least partly undertaken to out-compete others who seek the same goals. In a situation where everyone is an entrepreneur of and for themselves, any advantage one can get over anyone else is worth fighting for. If you're going for the same job as someone else with a similar level of experience, you need to mine that human capital to give yourself any competitive edge possible. Do you speak another language? Do you and the human resources department have any mutual acquaintances? Do your teeth look a little nicer, a little whiter and straighter, than your competitor's? Ultimately you can't be sure, so you need to maximise your human capital weeks, or months or years, ahead of time. The logic of continual self-improvement is baked into human capital, and any way one can improve oneself becomes a way of making oneself more profitable and more productive.

The connection between improvement and profit actually

goes all the way back to the origins of capitalism, so it's unsurprising that human capital implants these interests in our bodies and minds. In the seventeenth century, a literature of land improvement emerged in England, describing the various ways that agricultural land could be made more productive at the cost of eliminating small-scale farming and traditional farming techniques that had kept people fed for centuries.[20] Even the word "improve" has its etymological roots in profit-making, coming from the old French words *en* and *pros*, meaning "into" and "profit". Human capital takes this logic of improvement and profit-maximisation, central to capitalism, and ensures that people internalise it. Like a capitalist improving a field and ensuring a higher output in the future, any improvement we make to ourselves is a parallel increase in our human capital and is undertaken to grant us higher returns at a later date, even if it's years down the line.

It's for all these reasons that the current regime of ambition couldn't exist without the rise of human capital as a piece in the jigsaw puzzle of neoliberal subjectivity. We've been turned into capitalists of ourselves, and like any good capitalists, we have no choice but to compete against other capitalists lest we be left behind. Human capital changes ambition from a triumphant rising above obstacles into one more thing we need if we're to survive. And because unlike economic capital "the quantity of human capital is limitless", there's no end to the upward movement this competition demands.[21] Human capital as the reigning subjectivity of neoliberalism turns human life into a project of individualised, strategic, self-maximalisation, with promises of economic returns in the future. It's no wonder why everybody's ambitions trend towards entrepreneurship and business-owning. Human capital ensures that we're already entrepreneurs in waiting, and through following our ambitions we can supposedly discover our true potential.

But the matter goes deeper. Sculpting ambitious subjects out of the clay of human capital is ultimately a question of channelling people's desires, making them *want* certain things and attach their identities to a life they perceive as a self-fulfilling prophecy. Understanding how this is accomplished is the task of the rest of this chapter.

How to make people want something

The regular understanding of why we want things is based entirely on a sense of lack; as in, "I want a big car because the one I have now is too small", or "I want a relationship because I'm lonely", or "I want a new job because my boss is a prick." In examples such as these, the direction that desire takes — and it always has a direction, an object to strive towards — is determined by the things which the person lacks: a big car, someone to be with, a nicer boss.

Traditional psychoanalysis understands the desire-lack dyad in pretty much the same way. Freud and Lacan use concepts which rely on desires created by and directed towards something which the subject lacks naturally and seeks to acquire. Freud uses the concept of "penis envy" to describe the way people without penises experience this lack unconsciously in a way that structures their unconscious and directs their desires. This lack, Freud says, is the cause of female resentment from a young age, particularly towards the subjects' mothers, who supposedly failed to provide them with a penis in the womb. To come back to the idea of subjectivity, one could say that Freud understood female subjectivity as being defined, fundamentally, by this lack of a penis and their unconscious desire to recover a surrogate penis through whatever means possible.

Like Freud, Lacan's theory of psychoanalysis sees lack as absolutely fundamental to the human experience. Desire, the unconscious, personal fantasies and even the human subject are all founded upon an ontological lack, a lack of being, that can never be made complete.[22] Generations of ego psychologists argued that the path towards wellness for their patients (now more sensitively called "analysands") was to be found in mending their egos and attempting to cure them of their alienation. Lacan disagreed, arguing that the ego was nothing but a levee preventing people's true understanding of their lack to flood in, and that to reinforce the ego was a mistake, only clouding people's self-awareness further.[23] For Lacan, the lack at the heart of identity cannot be cured, and trying would only worsen one's psychological situation. This is echoed in his theory of sex. Whereas traditionalist theories of sex are founded upon the notion that sex should always be centred around reproduction — and someone like Foucault might see sex as an act of mutual pleasure — a Lacanian theory of sex might see the sex act as an attempt for two (or more) people to overcome their ontological lack, "a search for themselves by people who feel bereft of themselves".[24] In Lacan's highly pessimistic thought, we are little but alienated — fundamentally lacking — subjects on a quest to make ourselves complete, wanderers in a desert searching for an oasis that recedes as we get closer to it.

Deleuze and Guattari rebuke traditional psychoanalysis and what they call its "Platonic logic of desire" driven by a supposed lack lurking in the background of all things.[25] Against the *a priori* lack posited by Freud and Lacan, they argue that lack doesn't exist naturally; it has to be produced, *imposed*, and it's the imposition of lack that gives desire its direction.[26]

> The deliberate creation of lack as a function of market economy is the art of the dominant class. This involves deliberately organizing wants and needs [...] amid an abundance of production; making all of desire teeter and fall victim to the great fear of not having one's needs satisfied.[27]

In other words, the capitalist economy creates lack and scarcity, thereby "organizing wants and needs" and channelling our desires towards securing our ability to live. The creation of lack and scarcity imposes an object on our desires, constraining them within limits that are anything but natural. What Deleuze and Guattari call desiring-production — desire imagined as a factory — has no purpose but to flow freely, making connections without reference to an object in a process without a goal, much like Freud's description of infantile sexuality before things like penis envy came to dominate his theories. But the act of giving desire an object, a goal or an end towards which to aim, ensures that people will continue to struggle towards a determined outcome, towards the false hope of acquiring that which they lack. Again, from Deleuze and Guattari: "This welding of desire to lack is precisely what gives desire collective and personal ends, goals or intentions — instead of desire taken in the real order of its production, [...] devoid of any goal or intention."[28]

What does it mean to create lack? We assume that lack is the natural state of the world, and that it's actually abundance that needs to be intentionally created. (What else is the economy for?) But nothing could be further from the truth. A wonderful rebuttal to the existence of naturally occurring lack comes from an unexpected source: political anthropology. In an essay called "Society Against the State", Pierre Clastres wrote that so-called "primitive societies" don't lack anything. Contrary to our assumptions about them, these groups don't think of themselves as lacking; in fact, their social needs are met with far less work than we "civilised" people do every day. Clastres goes as far as to say that these stateless economies, which rely upon subsistence to meet their nutritional needs, outright refuse the excesses of a non-subsistence economy. Their lifestyles of hunting and gathering and foraging are not an unfortunate limitation of their technology — as we often see it — but are a deliberate choice of refusing any more than they need, which could easily give way to surplus resources, an economy to manage them and eventually more work. If "the only measure of how well a society is equipped in technology is its ability to meet its needs in a given environment", then the societies we deride as "primitive" were in fact doing just fine with the technology they had.[29] They weren't lacking anything; lack was imposed upon them by colonialists, even the "nice" ones who want to lift people out of their destitute conditions.

And yet, when these societies are described, they're usually described only in regard to what they lack when compared to us, a deeply ethnocentric line of thought.[30] They're only understood through reference to what they *don't* have, rather than what they do have: "societies *without* writing, societies *without* history".[31] Depending on what exact society is up for discussion, they might not have agriculture, like the Hadza in Tanzania; they might not have fixed dwellings, like many Bedouin in the Middle East and North Africa; or they might not have a written language, like many First Nations groups in the Americas and Australia prior to colonisation. As the title of his essay suggests, Clastres was an anarchist, so his primary focus was on how these "primitive" societies are characterised by their supposed lack of a state, a fixed centre of political power with a monopoly on the legitimate use of violence. The characterisation of these societies as *lacking* a state implies that they aren't fully complete — nor are they civilised — until they have one; they haven't moved far enough along the one-way evolution "from savagery to civilization".[32]

Some of Marx's most emphatic writing describes how capitalism came to be through the imposition of lack on feudal peasants. The driving of peasants from their communal properties forced them into a position where they had to sell their capacity to work — their labour power — if they wanted to survive. The feudal system allowed a proliferation of small-scale farms and people who could work on those farms and depend upon them for their basic subsistence. But the growth of capitalism ensured that small-scale farms were subsumed into larger and larger landholdings of capitalist farmers, and the peasants were removed from their small farms and "hurled onto the labour-market as free, unprotected and rightless proletarians".[33] At the same time, the size of personal gardens was dwindling, meaning that not only did people need to engage with the market for work, but they had to buy their food at the market as well.[34] This process lasted for centuries, and at its conclusion the peasants lacked the means by which to support their own existence without engaging with the market, and their desires were henceforth organised towards securing their most basic ability to live.

Marx's account focuses on men and the birth of the proletariat, but Marxist feminists have expanded this story to include women, and the removal of social agency imposed on them through similar processes. Silvia Federici's book *Caliban and the Witch* provides a history of how women came to be socially subordinate in around the same period as Marx's "primitive accumulation".[35] Since work was organised around subsistence agriculture on family farms, "no social separation existed between the production of goods and the reproduction of the workforce; all work contributed to the family's sustenance".[36] The domestic work that was typically done by women — raising children, cooking, cleaning, etc. — was equally socially useful as the more physically demanding farm work that was typically done by men, since both had their basis in reproducing, maintaining and sustaining the family and the community at large.

But this all changed with the advent of capitalist agriculture and the separation of the productive and reproductive spheres.[37] The work done by men — making tools, large-scale farming, the textile industry — created exchange value through the production of commodities to be sold at the market, and was the work from which business owners could extract a profit. The domestic labour done by women — in the service of reproducing the workforce — created use value but not exchange value, and went unpaid. Women's work was devalued, literally and figuratively, and women were cloistered in the domestic sphere, without even the money to support themselves that their husbands received from working on the emerging capitalist farms or factories. The emergence of capitalism uniquely imposed a lack of social agency and autonomy on women that hasn't yet disappeared, nor will it entirely disappear until the end of capitalism at the very least.[38] And it is *this* lack that women are responding to via Freudian "penis envy", not the crude biological fact of having been born with a vagina rather than a penis.[39]

It's been hundreds of years since primitive accumulation and the lack it imposed on the peasants, but the artificial lack under capitalism hasn't gone away. Most notably in major cities' homelessness and food crises, the lack of human necessities is maintained for profit. In almost every global city today, there are more homes left empty than there are homeless people. Between holiday homes remaining unused for half the year, long-term rentals being turned into AirBnBs and put on short-term leases for an absurd markup, homes and apartments intentionally left vacant to manufacture scarcity or to ensure a slightly larger profit upon sale of other properties, and the rise of luxury housing unaffordable to the majority of working-class people, my country of Australia had more than a million properties totally vacant upon the recent census in 2022, empty housing for about 4% of Australia's population.[40] Those who don't want to see the housing market changed or houses distributed differently have ready-made rejoinders to this statistic: "What about the owners renovating their homes?" "What about competitive real estate markets?" "What about small mum-and-dad investors who depend on their housing investment income for a living?" But this is exactly what Deleuze and Guattari refer to as lack created by social production. This isn't always a group of greedy individuals doing whatever they can get away with; for the most part, anyway, these are the results of the capitalist economy creating and maintaining lack, as it has done from the very outset.

The artificial lack we see in housing is also present in another basic human necessity: food. Like housing, there is enough food to satisfy everyone's needs, but excess food is thrown away to maintain profit margins. The profitable discarding of both food and housing can be understood through "abject capital", a term coined by David Giles, an old anthropology teacher of mine. Abject capital refers to "those once-commodities that are still useful but that are more profitable to throw away than to sell".[41] A vast quantity of food found in dumpsters is perfectly edible, but for whatever reason — visual imperfections, a minor bruise, bad luck on behalf of the produce, etc. — it is no longer seen as sellable or profitable, and is worth more thrown out than it is taking up space on supermarket shelves. David liked to demonstrate this by making banana bread when he was giving talks or teaching classes for the first time. He would only tell us that he got the bananas from a dumpster after we'd already had a few mouthfuls, demonstrating just how edible the produce is, despite its apparent transition from commodity to refuse. (In fact, experienced bakers already know that overripe bananas are actually better for baking than the bright yellow ones found on supermarket shelves. So, if you want to make banana bread without rifling through a dumpster, prepare to have some bananas slowly blackening on your kitchen table.) Quite early in his ethnography of dumpster diving, David offers a photo of a well-known dumpster in Seattle, which held nothing but chocolate.[42] As with housing, food's status as abject capital has to be maintained through some degree of force. Just as squatting is an illegal and marginalised practice, dumpster diving is often prevented by supermarkets with padlocks and chains, and by police with more aggressive means if they feel it's necessary.

All this is to show that *of course lack exists*, but lack is created and maintained through the mechanisms of capitalism and the state; it's by no means a natural condition. This is precisely what Deleuze and Guattari mean when they say that "lack is created, planned, and organized in and through social production."[43] It would seem as though surplus and abundance are in fact the natural condition and have to be curtailed for the sake of the economy. There is more food than we can eat, and more housing than homeless, but natural abundance simply isn't profitable.

The point of all of this is that ambition is like any other desire under capitalism; it is constrained, channelled and repressed through lack. Desire can never be freed while food, housing and other basic necessities are withheld to secure profits. Where Deleuze and Guattari's conception of desire has no goal but to make connections, where desire is a productive force not aimed towards accomplishing anything, ambition is the result of organised desire towards the ends of neoliberal capitalism. So, the question remains: If ambitious desires are created by imposing lack, what do we lack that creates ambition?

Alienation: a lack of control and recognition

In one of Marx's early works, he introduces his spin on the older Hegelian concept of "alienation".[44] In Hegel's work, alienation usually refers to part of the process by which a subject becomes fully self-conscious, but Marx — typical for him — uses alienation to describe the ways that capitalism uniquely separates us from the things around us. In other words, he uses alienation as a social concept, rather than a religious or philosophical one.[45] Marx argues that capitalism alienates people from the rest of their world in four ways: from others; from our natural inclination for acting in the environment (Marx calls this humans' "species-essence"); from our engagement in the process of production; and finally, from the products made in that process. The forms of alienation most relevant here are those last two, where the workers experience a lack of control over how they work and the products of their work, and a lack of social recognition for the work they've done.

As we've seen already, in the feudal system, people worked in farms and workshops mostly on a subsistence basis, and with the aim of reproducing their families and their local communities. If a group of people ate some bread and they themselves didn't bake it, they would likely know the names of the people who harvested that wheat and baked the bread — they might even know them personally as well. The same is true of the other side; the people harvesting the wheat and baking the bread would be doing so obviously out of some necessity — they still need to eat to live — but they wouldn't be directed to do so by a boss, and they would probably have some say over where the wheat went and how the bread itself was made. Moreover, they could do their job whenever and however they liked, so long as the bread eventually got made for people to eat.

Things are very different in the work process today, whether one is pulling levers in a factory, sweating over a deep fryer or typing away in an office. For all the ways work has changed in the last few centuries since the advent of capitalism, the people doing the work have continued to lack control and recognition for their labour. Let's use two different kinds of work within the same company as examples: a production manager and an advertising copywriter, both of whom work for McDonald's. A production manager walks the floors of factories and warehouses, ensuring that the particular way those cardboard burger boxes are folded is all going according to plan. The copywriter, on the other hand, is sitting in an office (or at home), spitballing potential advertising slogans for a new ad campaign or writing those self-congratulatory messages that go on the side of the brown paper bags. Though these people have very different jobs, they both sell their labour power to McDonald's, and neither of them has any real control over how they work, nor to what end their labour goes. Moreover, the results of both of these workers' labour aren't described as work *they* did but as work

McDonald's did. *McDonald's* ensures their supply chains run on schedule; *McDonald's* writes mindfulness affirmations and environmental awareness messages on their brown paper bags. When a worker sells their labour time to a capitalist, they also sell the recognition for their work being done, and that belongs to the capitalist as well, or at least the company for which the person works. Or, in Marx's words, "Just as [the worker] estranges from himself his own activity, so he confers to the stranger activity which is not his own".[46]

As conservative commentators gleefully remind us, Marx never worked in any of the factories he described; he never faced the conditions of industrial capitalism in the same way workers did. But some labour psychology research suggests his analysis of workers' alienation is fairly solid more than a century later. Researchers in the US ran an experiment in which they tried to isolate the sense of alienation participants felt in performing a menial task.[47] All the participants shared a task: they were to build Lego models to instruction. They were paid $2 for the first model completed, and their pay reduced by $0.11 for each model built. Participants were split into two groups: "Meaningful" and "Sisyphus". In the Meaningful group, participants' finished Lego models would be placed in front of them, and as the experiment went on, the participant could see how many models he'd made (all the participants were male). In the aptly named "Sisyphus" group, participants' finished models would be disassembled in front of them, and they would then make another model with the exact same pieces. Confirming one's intuitions, those in the Meaningful group, whose labour was designed to be less alienated from its products than that of the Sisyphus group, were willing to assemble more Lego models for less money, suggesting that

Marx's theory of alienation isn't merely random speculation but that it has a material effect on workers.[48]

These same labour psychology experimenters ran another test. This time, they tested the degree to which being recognised for one's work affects one's willingness to work. The task this time involved the participants being given a sheet of paper with random letter sequences on it, and they were given $0.55 each time they found ten sets of consecutive letters. Once they finished the first sheet, they were asked if they'd be willing to complete a second sheet for $0.50, then a third sheet for $0.45, and on and on it went. This time the experimenters split the participants into three categories: Acknowledged, who wrote their names on the sheets of paper; Ignored, who weren't asked to write their name; and Shredded, whose sheets of paper would immediately be shredded upon completion, without the researchers even looking at the finished work. One might expect the violence of immediately shredding someone's work to make it the outlying category, but there was very little difference in the results between the Ignored group and the Shredded group, with an average of 6.77 and 6.34 sheets completed per person, respectively. It was in fact the Acknowledged group that was the outlier, which finished an average of 9.03 sheets per person, and half the group continued their work until the pay reached zero. The manner in which someone's work went unrecognised was relatively unimportant compared to the simple fact that it went unrecognised at all.

I'm a little suspicious of labour psychology's motives, because the entire purpose of the field is to figure out ways to get people to work more for less money. But the results of these experiments nonetheless provide valuable insights into alienation and the labour process, despite the ends the research is eventually put to. Even though the tasks performed in these experiments have no inherent meaning — assembling Lego figurines and finding consecutive letters in a random sequence — they can be made more or less meaningful by additional factors, like the participants having some ownership of the completed work and making a noticeable effect on the world, and being recognised for the work they have done. So despite his lack of experience working in the factories of Victorian England, it seems as though Marx wasn't far off the mark when he lamented how "the worker is related to the *product of his labour* as to an *alien* object".[49]

When we're outside of work, we often try to find ways of overcoming the alienation we experience while we're at work. This could help explain why, in the early days of the Covid pandemic, people lucky enough to be working from home seemed to be baking loaf upon loaf of sourdough bread. Explanations for the rise of home baking during Covid tend to focus on elements of distraction, or scientific control, or sustainable production, or just good quality bread.[50] And while I'm not discounting those factors, what seemingly goes uncommented upon is that baking bread — and all personal cooking, as a matter of fact — is a sure-fire way of having your labour recognised as something *you* have done and contains a noticeable element of the work *you* have personally put in. Those of us who voluntarily cook for partners, friends or family can attest to the difference between that activity and the compelled work done for money.

Ambition is a desire to overcome the alienation of work, the lack of recognition and control over how one spends forty or more hours a week, in ways other than engaging in extra-work activities or changing the structure of *all* work, as the left have traditionally sought to do. Ambition channels the desire to transcend one's individual alienation towards industry success, de-alienating one's own work by climbing to the top of the food chain, where one will have control and be socially recognised. I'm reminded of a joke told by the stand-up comedian Bill Burr following the death of Apple founder Steve Jobs. Burr joked that the people actually making tech innovations at Apple were a series of "nameless, faceless scientists", and that amidst all the hype about his personal genius, Jobs ultimately "told other people what to invent".[51] Burr follows this observation up by strutting around the stage, pretending to be Jobs, screaming "Get on it!" at the workers around him, before remarking upon how Jobs would invariably end up on conference stages alone, as a solitary genius. Jobs's ambition clearly paid off, he's still remembered more than a decade after his death for beginning Apple and supposedly bringing it to success single-handedly. Sure, those "nameless, faceless scientists" Burr describes get to feel some of the sense that they've changed the tech world — inventing the iPhone is nothing to sneeze at. But Apple is popularly understood to be Jobs's creation, and his alone.

This is where that ambition for individual entrepreneurship that I mentioned in the last chapter comes back into the picture. Entrepreneurship, no matter on how small a scale it occurs, is unalienated by its very nature. Not only does the entrepreneur live by the assumption that they're free, since they act as their own boss, but they no longer relate to the products of their labour as "alien objects", as something outside and against themselves.[52] Whether they own a gift shop, create an app or own and work in a food truck, entrepreneurs are recognised for their labour. And not only are they recognised for their labour in a way many of us aren't, but, as in the case of Jobs above, entrepreneurs and small-business owners are often recognised for the labour of others. They've escaped workplace alienation, at least for as long as their enterprise stays afloat.

It's worth saying that I'm of course implicated in all this as well. One of the appeals of writing is that it's one of the least alienated activities that can still be considered a job. My name is on the cover of this book, and the few articles I've written here or there have my name on the byline, so people can recognise me through some of the work I've done. The production supervisor overseeing cardboard at the McDonald's factory can't see any of himself or his "free, conscious activity" in the results of his labour, but I can see something of myself in the books I've written, and others can as well. The vast majority of the writing on the internet is done for either very little pay or none at all, and I fully believe that the unalienated nature of writing is a reason why the online culture industry is largely upheld by writing done for free. No one writes death metal album reviews because they're after fame and fortune. Writing on the internet for free could be considered the same kind of unalienated activity outside of work as the example of baking during Covid. It's only once you start writing books that your work gets wrapped up in the trappings of personal entrepreneurship.

A lack of control and recognition prevails over almost everything we do while we're at work. While we can try to find ways of overcoming or avoiding alienation outside the workplace, ultimately we're bound by the social conditions set by neoliberal capitalism, and will attempt to work within these conditions to the best of our ability. Ambition is the result: an individualised striving towards an unalienated life while remaining firmly within the bounds set by a system that seems impossible to change.

Entrepreneurial models and model entrepreneurs
Creating a lack to fill isn't the only step in the production of ambitious subjects. Stoking someone's ambition requires

more than putting them in a miserable position and crossing your fingers. No, the production of ambition requires a positive element, something to stoke that sense of self-affirmation so crucial to neoliberal subjectivity. An array of models, supposedly successful cases of ambition paying off, provides one such positive element.

"The precondition for any ambition is the representation of a real or imaginary model that the individual desires to realize."[53] In other words, to be ambitious is necessarily to follow a path someone has trekked before you, even unconsciously. The psychologist James Hillman conceptualises the soul as an acorn which "needs models for its mimesis" to grow into the metaphorical oak tree.[54] For Hillman, these are our personal heroes and heroines, who "provide the ectypes on earth that release the guiding archetypes of the soul".[55] In other words, what Hillman calls our souls or our acorns contain archetypes that put us on a certain path, and our personal heroes and heroines are earthly manifestations of those transcendental archetypes whose lives we can use as motivation.[56] We will deviate from the path these models set, Hillman concedes, but we still require people worth mimicking.

How many teenagers watched the Nineties slacker film *Clerks* with their friends and immediately bought the cheapest camera they could get their hands on, seeking to emulate the director? Apropos of that old story, how many people saw the Velvet Underground and started bands of their own? How many start-up hopefuls model themselves on the likes of Steve Jobs? Elizabeth Holmes of Theranos is the most infamous, but the number is surely enormous. The models one chooses don't have to be as dramatic as those in the arts. If somebody sees an older family member starting their own business, they're more likely to see themselves as someone who could realistically start a business of their own. They personally know somebody who has risen the ranks to become a member of the petty bourgeoisie, so they understand that the possibility for their family is a possibility for them also.

The ways in which we imitate people are mostly unconscious, and who we might gravitate towards is a matter of sheer chance.[57] But occasionally role models are propped up and maintained for the sake of creating behaviour considered to be socially beneficial. Australia famously outperforms in sporting events, considering its meagre population size, so sportspeople have a lot of influence in public discourse in Australia. One of the tasks the Australian Institute of Sport gives its Olympians is to visit schools and talk to children about how they became elite sportspeople and what they had to do to achieve that goal.[58] On one hand, these visits are supposed to inspire children to put more effort into sport and hopefully become professional athletes, one of the few avenues of social mobility for the working class in Australia. On the other hand, the talks given by the sportspeople invariably stress the same personality traits and strategies of self-management so common in neoliberal culture: taking individual responsibility, ascetic sacrifice for a future goal, self-discipline, dreaming big, actualising your infinite potential, no matter your obstacles. It's no wonder why the Australian government might lean on sportspeople to repeat the essential neoliberal values to children. Using athletes as life-models shows children that they too have the capacity to achieve their dreams, so long as they're willing to become good students and workers at the same time.

As of late, some internet personalities have made quite a lot of money by positioning themselves as role models, particularly to teenage boys and young men. The rise of these self-help motivational entrepreneurs provides people with images of lives that are not their own, and these motivators almost always sell courses geared towards teaching young people how to live lives like theirs. Tai Lopez and Gary Vaynerchuk (or "Gary Vee", as he calls himself) could be considered the old guard of this particular genre of influencing, but they've been well and truly eclipsed by Andrew Tate, former kickboxer and current alleged sex trafficker. All three men traffic in education, making their fortunes by selling either online courses or tickets to in-person seminars. At time of writing, the first thing one sees on Tai Lopez's website is a massive banner ad for one of his seminars. Tate's online program, the Real World — formerly Hustlers University[59] — teaches people how to earn passive income online through cryptocurrency trading, dropshipping (more flatteringly called "e-commerce") and copywriting using AI.[60] By absorbing their lessons, these courses imply, one will be able to live the same kind of lavish lifestyle as Lopez, Vaynerchuk or Tate.

Entrepreneurs and businesspeople have often given advice to their admirers. Benjamin Franklin's "Advice to a Young Tradesman" is one of the most famous texts of early American capitalism.[61] But Franklin didn't sell his advice as a pamphlet on every street corner. The innovation of the likes of Lopez, Vaynerchuk and Tate is that they all cash in on the turn towards human capital and its promotion of "lifelong learning", monetising their business advice any way they can. From the other side, these men's fans support them monetarily *for* that advice. Nobody hires a mechanic to fix their car because they want to be a mechanic, but legions of teenage boys spend their money on courses by the likes of Tate, Lopez and Vaynerchuk specifically to learn lessons about how to emulate them and their lives most effectively.

Tate had two main innovations which set him above Lopez and Vaynerchuk in the competition for overly online young men's attention; only the latter am I able to properly analyse here: the first is his full-throated embrace of right-wing politics; the second is his style of relating to his fans by not relating at all. Lopez and Vaynerchuk don't hesitate to revel in conspicuous consumption, showing off their fancy cars and impressive houses, but Tate is the only one who would explicitly criticise his fans for being losers, a term he uses to no small effect. Over and over again, Tate describes the ways in which his life is so much better and more interesting than those of his viewers: he's always surrounded by beautiful women; he drives expensive cars; he takes luxury holidays in exotic locales. We've seen all this before, of course, in everything from Instagram influencers to Jordan Belfort and his larger-than-life "Wolf of Wall Street" personality. But as I've said, Tate's innovation is in making the difference between his life and those of his viewers, their lack relative to his, so apparent, and in such an in-your-face way.

Chantal Jaquet writes that the production of ambitious desire requires a sense of dissatisfaction with oneself and one's origins:

> The vague desire for a different life, which is presupposed by the orientation towards a different model from those that prevail, can only arise if there is dissatisfaction, even suffering. The person who feels perfectly happy and suited to their milieu does not long to leave it, and is less open to encounters of friendship or love that might upend her world.[62]

Creating dissatisfaction and "vague desire for a different life" is what Tate does best, flaunting his consumption and emphasising his audience's lack of money so much that they can't help but be miserable when they consider their own situations. They internalise Tate's ideals and view themselves "with the eyes of others" much richer than themselves.[63] Tate's business model requires his audience to be dissatisfied with themselves and their lives so he can prop himself and his life up as the solution.

What these motivational entrepreneurs accomplish, besides using a sketchy business model to enrich themselves before others can join in on the racket, is to offer an image of a life; a singular idea of how a life is supposed to be led and an implicit invalidation of all other ways of life. The suggestion, occasionally made explicit, is that if you aren't striving to live like Andrew Tate, or if you try to replicate his lifestyle and fail, your life isn't really worth living.

Conclusion

In short, making people ambitious requires a constellation of factors coming together at once. As per the last chapter, it needs a social system which encourages ambition and an economic system which makes social mobility at least theoretically possible. It requires people to engage with the market in order to acquire basic necessities, and to lack autonomy and social recognition in lower-status jobs so that their desires are constrained within the limits set by reclaiming these things they lack. It needs one to understand one's own life as both a result and an ongoing process of investments over which one was in total control, so one can strategise their social mobility the way a stock manager organises a portfolio. And finally, it requires one have a tangible model to replicate, to strive towards: a target who appears to lack nothing. This isn't the end of the story, though. So much hinges upon how successful one is in their ambitious quest, and how well they can replicate their chosen model. This is the subject of the next chapter.

4. On Failure

Achievement society creates depressives and losers.
— Byung-Chul Han, *The Burnout Society*[1]

It's a freedom in admitting it's not gonna get better.
— billy woods, "Remorseless"

French philosopher Paul Virilio once argued that every invention is the simultaneous invention of a new kind of accident. The invention of the car was also the invention of the multi-car pile-up. The invention of the train was also the invention of derailment. The invention of the smart phone was the invention of smart phone addiction. The previous chapter tackled the production of ambitious neoliberal subjects who understand their lives as a process of self-investment. This chapter will cover the often unacknowledged accidents ambition creates: dashed hopes, failed projects, ideas which refuse to get off the ground, bad investments and a class of people socially recognised to be failures. Failure is to ambition what the Chernobyl disaster is to the nuclear reactor.

Like it or not, failure is an inevitable part of ambition. Once our lives are stamped with a telos — that grand sense of one's ultimate purpose I wrote about in Chapter 1 — we introduce the possibility that we'll fail to achieve that purpose, and suffer the results. When we set out to mimic successful people whose ambition has paid off, we can never mimic them as much as we'd like to, nor will we ever be able to totally replicate their success. The problem with seeing yourself as a copy of another, or another as a copy of yourself, is that there will always be a slippage between the two. It's inevitable. Photocopiers never produce an exact replication of whatever it is they're copying; there's always something missing in the margins, or some dust indelibly printed onto the copy that can be brushed off the original.[2] In a world conceivable only in terms of copies and originals, ectypes and archetypes, models and mimics, the copies are destined to be nothing more than inadequate versions of the originals.

Practically speaking, this should all be fairly obvious. Nobody can ever mimic someone else entirely, but that doesn't stop people from trying. Aspiring athletes always look to the athletes who came before them, as do entrepreneurs and artists. The story we tell ourselves about individual achievements — that our predecessors' success came from them and them alone — is a comfort here, because it means that the only thing we need to emulate is their learned skills and perseverance, which are things we can emulate with a lot of hard work. Ignoring all the broader details of successful people's lives — their family background, education, social position, socioeconomic status, etc. — fools us into thinking that the *only* thing separating us from the most successful people in society is how much we're willing to sacrifice on the road to greatness. In the vast majority of cases, that just isn't true.

If mimicry is a doomed enterprise, then that would mean failure is a near constant. Yet why do we never seem to hear about it? I think the obvious explanation — the survivor's fallacy — is probably the correct one. If someone's life hasn't gone well, either due to social limits or what is perceived to be their own incompetence, they aren't going to be given deals to write or produce a book or a movie about their experiences, nor will they want to. If someone does get given a book deal, to etch into the public record their own rags-to-riches story, their initial failings will be used as examples of the value of perseverance, of the struggle for individual greatness, no matter one's obstacles.

Another reason failure isn't as well known is because failure is often not compelling in a narratological sense. The sociologist Susie Scott has developed what she's called the "sociology of nothing" as a way of highlighting the effect failure has. She turns her analysis towards "people, objects and actions that conspicuously fail to emerge in social life" to show us that failure, much as we might pretend otherwise, is omnipresent.[3] The world is full of things we haven't done, identities that've failed to develop. One of Scott's research participants describes the phenomenon perfectly:

> I often — weekly? — think about the lives I am not living and will never live. The life where I became an artist, rather than a psychologist. The life where I didn't have children. The life where I took the job in Michigan instead of the one in Oregon (yikes!). The life where I recognized my passions earlier […]. I think there was a point in my early twenties, when I stood on the precipice of adulthood, and all the possibilities really did seem open to me. It was hard, in my early thirties, to recognize that the moment had passed.[4]

These non-occurrences make up a large part of our inner lives, but they don't make compelling narratives. Stories are about *what happens*, not the endless possibilities which could have happened. Your fantasies about choosing one relationship over another, moving to a different part of the country or the world, might be compelling, but they make better stories to tell on a therapist's couch than on a movie screen.

A final reason failure is so rarely discussed in popular culture is that it pierces the veil of our societies, which encourage aspiration and ambition as a panacea for all our class-based problems. Those who would claim that a lack of ambition is the primary problem of the working class — the UK's New Labour government of the early 2000s used the term "poverty of aspiration" to describe this supposed problem[5] — have nothing to say in response to the glaringly obvious possibility of failure, because widespread failure would mean that there are deeper and broader issues at hand than instilling in children the desire to aim high. These promoters of ambition would rather publicise the extremely rare cases of upward social mobility, and hide the much more common cases of *downward* social mobility, than make broad structural changes to benefit society's least well-off.

For these reasons, I want to highlight a few stories about failure, in part to emphasise the way ambition often has negative consequences that are so rarely discussed, but also to show how failure can be a springboard to unexpected political possibilities.

Failure and its consequences

I spent years of my life feeling like a failure. After graduating high school with ever-so-slightly above-average grades — which I was assured would've been higher if I'd ever managed to apply myself more studiously — I took a year off from school and worked full time at a local supermarket. When a year passed and it came time to go to university, I lasted a grand total of four days before packing it in. My heart wasn't in it. So I worked at that same supermarket for the next few years, spending my free time hanging out with my friends, saving money to go overseas, and occasionally experimenting with drugs.

It sometimes surprises people when I tell them that I actually quite *enjoyed* my time working at that supermarket. They often baulk at the suggestion that I could be happy while working a job with so little cultural cache (this was long before Covid and the nominal gratitude "essential workers" were granted by those lucky enough to work from home). But I worked on my feet, with my friends, and got a lot of exercise while making decent-enough money.

Of course, after a while, feelings of inadequacy came leaking in. This was less because of *my* opinion of the work I was doing, and more about the way in which what I was doing was talked about by some people I knew. A fairly common interaction went like this: Someone would ask me what I was doing with myself, and I would tell them the broad strokes of my work. Then, they'd make a comment implying that I was "wasting my potential" in some way, with the insinuation that the work I was doing was beneath me and that I should be moving onto bigger and better things. Before these interactions, I certainly wasn't ambitious, but I didn't really feel like a failure either. It was only due to the repetition of these interactions that I came to think of myself as a failure. I'd been "hailed" as a failure, in the Althusserian sense, and ideas of myself as a failure began to creep in.

It was only a couple of years later that I managed to find some — thankfully, not all — of my own experiences reflected back to me, in a recent Australian book set just a few kilometres from where I was living at the time. Christos Tsiolkas's novel *Barracuda* is about failure. Better put, one could say it's about ambition and social mobility, and what happens when these things don't go our way.

Barracuda's protagonist is Danny Kelly, the son of a Scottish father and a Greek mother, growing up in the inner north of Melbourne in the 1990s, before gentrification would come to turn that area into an archipelago of vintage clothes shops and overpriced cafes. Danny is nicknamed "Barracuda" because he has a knack for swimming, so much so that his athletic achievements win him a scholarship to an expensive boys-only private high school, which co-ed public school Danny and his best friend Demet call "Cunts College".[6] Despite their world-class coaching, expensive equipment and wealthy families, Danny's new swim team don't stand a chance against him, and he quickly makes a name for himself as a young Olympic contender.

Like a lot of stories about upward social mobility, *Barracuda* goes to great lengths to show Danny developing a sense of shame about his family and the social class to which his family belongs. Danny can't help but be embarrassed when his mother watches his first training session at his new school, but the situation goes far beyond the way every teenager is invariably embarrassed by their parents. "He'd been embarrassed by her before [...]. But he'd never been ashamed, he'd never wanted her to *fuck off* before."[7] What Danny feels isn't the familial embarrassment every teenager feels. He feels a *class* embarrassment. Danny understands that his mother's presence articulates just how much he doesn't belong at his new high school, especially compared to his schoolmates who have been preparing to go to "Cunts College" all their lives. : Later in the novel, when Danny wins a national Under-16s swimming competition, Demet offers to take him to McDonald's to celebrate his victory, and Danny is embarrassed simply by imagining what his new schoolmates would think: "Taylor would be in stitches, Scooter would be on the floor. He could hear them: *They're taking you to Macca's? To celebrate? Are you serious, fucking Macca's?*"[8] In the previous chapter, I highlighted Chantal Jaquet's point that ambition can't exist without a sense of dissatisfaction at one's family background such that the ambitious person can rise above it, and how ambition is often created by stoking this dissatisfaction. This example brings it into sharp relief, showing how Danny's dissatisfaction is a product of his new private school environment.

Danny rises through the ranks of his local competitions with almost no resistance. But his self-assuredness and natural talent lead to his first setback having oversized consequences. When Danny finishes fourth in an Olympic qualifying event in Japan, he has a complete meltdown while still in the pool, lashing out at his competitors, his teammates and his coach, and refuses to swim competitively again. And unlike his teammates, swimming is the only thing Danny has to grant him even the possibility of social mobility. While others at his school have family investments, networking connections, highly paid teachers and university spots to act as golden parachutes, Danny doesn't have any of that. So when he falls, he falls hard. He bullies other students at "Cunts College" to regain a sliver of dignity, becomes socially isolated and later takes to alcohol to cope with constantly seeing himself as a failure. On the night of the Olympics opening ceremony — the Olympics Danny was aiming to win — Danny drunkenly crashes a party thrown by a former swimming teammate and beats him half to death.

To better understand the pathological kind of failure Danny experiences, we can turn to the anarchist philosopher Max

Stirner and his idiosyncratic theory of property. For Stirner, property is based on a law of the ancient Romans which states that to truly *own* something is to have total sovereignty over it, meaning that one must also have the ability to destroy or dispose of it at will: "*ius utendi et abutendi re sua, quatenus iuris ratio patitur*".[9] If the law prevents someone from destroying their property, then it's not truly theirs but the state's, and those who purport to own it are merely caretakers of it. It follows that if someone can't destroy their property because of their own attachment to it, then it's not truly their property either. The relationship has beeen inverted, and the object has dominion over the person unable to destroy it. This relationship is what characterises Stirner's notion of "fixed ideas", ideas that have become so thoroughly inculcated that they hold dominion over a person: "an idea that has subjected people to itself".[10] The person lives to serve the idea, rather than the other way around.

This is certainly true of Danny's condition for much of *Barracuda*, as he continues to obsess about his failure long after the event, unable to destroy the idea of himself as an Olympian, and unable to properly move on from the ambition that has been inculcated in him by himself and everyone around him since he was a child. He moves through the novel as a ghost, resentful of the person who he might've been had things gone differently. He comes to resemble Francis Bacon's vivid picture of an ambitious person whose hopes have been dashed: a person of extreme resentment, hostile to the outside world and willing to destroy others to please himself. If ambitious people's desires go unfulfilled, Bacon writes, "they become secretly discontent, and look upon men and matters with an evil eye, and are best pleased, when things go backward".[11] The apex of Danny's resentment and hostility occurs during the opening ceremony of the Olympics because his fixed idea of himself as an Olympian reminds him over and over that, if not for his failure, he would've been there and likely would have won.

As poignant as it is, *Barracuda* is ultimately a work of fiction, and as a story of working-class sportsmanship it is specific to its Australian context. If we want a non-fiction parallel to Tsiolkas's novel, Wendy Liu's part-critique part-memoir *Abolish Silicon Valley* fits the bill.[12] Similar to *Barracuda*, Liu's book is a story about one's individual ambitions brushing against massive structural limitations and individual discontents. *Abolish Silicon Valley* begins by describing her actual desire, before it becomes channelled by capitalism into a path which others have already taken. A product of hacker culture and open-source software, Liu was interested in the less commercial side of computer programming from a young age. She did idolise certain famous Silicon Valley founders, of course, like Steve Jobs and Bill Gates, but mostly in their early periods, when they were building software, not so much when they became CEOs responsible for managing massive companies, maximising profit and buying up competitors. Eventually, Liu's skills and an internal referral get her a prized position as a summer intern at Google. Everything seems to be on the up and up.

Quickly, Liu's internship begins to seem like a trap, just another corporate gig among a million others, if one with generous pay and benefits. Google's motto of "Don't be evil" starts to ring hollow when Liu witnesses Larry Page and Sergey Brin making light of a recent firing during an announcement to employees. Moreover, she becomes more and more disillusioned with Google's supposed generosity when she realises that their vast army of temporary and outsourced labour — the cleaners, security, hospitality staff and company bus drivers — aren't given the same benefits as even the summer interns like herself.[13] They don't get the free accommodation in ultra-pricey San Francisco, nor the free sushi.

After all this, Liu and a few friends set out to make a start-up of their own, convinced that they can be the next big thing without sacrificing their ethical standards. In trying to continue programming for the love of the game, her group set out without a coherent business model, only an underlying technical infrastructure and a goal to make it big. Of course, start-ups *are* a business, and here we can see how the project was probably doomed from the very beginning, but Liu makes it clear that she was still a programmer at heart, not a businessperson.

A crucial moment in the memoir occurs when Liu and her crew read a profile of a start-up much like theirs.

The piece detailed the founders' gradual lowering of their aims, from their initial sky-high ambition to build something world-changing into finding themselves creating a banal e-commerce plugin based on the advice of their investors. Not only did they not become millionaires, but the autonomy they thought they had as founders was only illusory, a shroud to conceal the truth of a system primarily benefiting those who already had money.[14]

Though she admits reading the piece affected her more than she expected, Liu says she got past her hang-ups by convincing herself that she founded one of the handful of start-ups to become successful in the long-term. But, as you might expect, it all went to shit over time. Capitulations to the ever-shifting tech market led to a fatal dilution of the group's goals, and they simply weren't as good at chasing money as the other start-ups they found themselves competing against. Not willing to lower themselves to the e-commerce sphere, they disbanded completely and gave up on their start-up dream.

Compared to the height of their ambitions, Danny Kelly and Wendy Liu could both be considered failures, given they both failed to accomplish their stated goals. Rather than an Olympic swimmer, Danny ends up working in a supermarket and, by the end of his story, becomes a disability support worker; and rather than becoming the next Steve Jobs, Liu ends up a programmer and a writer on tech culture. No matter how necessary disability support is, and no matter how much I liked Liu's book, neither of these books' protagonists succeeded in their actual, stated goals. Even though their settings and time periods are very different, and their protagonists take different paths out of failure, the books complement each other as necessary depictions of failure, why failure is so common, and the feelings that go along with it.

But failure doesn't just make people miserable; on a broader level it also serves the interests of capital, even if unintentionally, in two crucial ways. The first is that if one is sufficiently ambitious to feel the sting of failure, they will have invested so much time, money and energy into their goal that they'll be completely untrained and unskilled in anything else, and thus easily replaceable by another who's equally untrained and unskilled. If one has spent a decade trying to become a painter in the fine arts and it doesn't work out, they lack the specialisation and money necessary to build a life. Danny from *Barracuda* spends his entire high school experience attempting to become a gold-medallist swimmer for Australia, and when he fails, he's left without the skills or training for anything else. (And after burning his private school bridges, he doesn't have any social capital to fall back on, either.) This is why, after all his expensive private schooling, he ends up working night shifts at a local supermarket. Everyone else his age will have specialised in some way, either gone to university or found their own place in the division of labour. But Danny has done neither; he sacrificed all of that on the altar of his future success, and his failure leaves him without even the corner he painted himself into.

If Wendy Liu hadn't become a writer and a critic of the tech industry, she could very easily have become a programmer for Google or Apple or any number of major tech companies after her start-up collapsed, competing against other programmers for a limited number of tech jobs. One could argue that's a more skilled profession than a lot of the jobs we call "unskilled", and that's true, but with the current encroachment of AI into the tech sphere, even computer programmers are at risk of being deskilled, and the programmers who aren't let go are becoming supervisors of work done by AI rather than doing the majority of the work themselves.[15]

I've worked supermarket jobs like the one Danny Kelly ends up in after failing to qualify for the Olympics, and even though the work can be physically exhausting and some people can do the job better than others, there's nonetheless a sense that anyone could do it with a minimal amount of training. This is precisely the critique of capitalism's tendency to deskill labour: it serves the interests of management by constantly reminding workers that they can easily be replaced, since a work process that doesn't require skilled workers can have high turnover with little economic downside. New workers can be taken on by a company with little training besides the management of machinery, and supervisors can threaten to fire workers if they fall behind and replace them with workers as deskilled as themselves.[16] Marx cites a man who states the matter plainly:

> The factory operatives should keep in wholesome remembrance the fact that theirs is really a low species of skilled labour; and that there is none which is more easily acquired, or of its quality more amply renumerated, or which by a short training of the least expert can be more quickly, as well as abundantly, acquired.[17]

To put it more succinctly: a lack of skills makes workers easily replaceable, and constant reminders of that fact are an effective method of keeping wayward workers in line.

The second reason failure benefits capital is psychological. If someone considers themselves a failure, chances are they'll lack confidence in both the world and themselves — unable to imagine a better world as well as disbelieving in their ability to accomplish their goals. If someone fails at their goals of becoming a concert pianist or a Formula One driver or a successful influencer due to their own perceived lack of ability or will, they become very aware of their inability to act on the world in a way that conforms to their desires. To paraphrase Spinoza, the difference between *hope* and *confidence* is that the former comes with an element of doubt; confidence is a hope without any reason to doubt one's success.[18] A large enough failure gives one a reason to doubt one's capacity, a fact we also see in *Barracuda*. After Danny quits swimming, he takes driving lessons to get his license, but he takes them secretly because "he could fail. He could stall, he could forget the requisite three seconds at a stop sign; something simple like that could mean a fail and he must not fail."[19] This internal monologue is a far cry from the self-assured, confident person Danny used to be, gliding through the water with no resistance — psychological or physical. The prose repeats the word "could" to draw attention to Danny's doubt in his own abilities, and rather than striving for success as he used to, he focuses instead on avoiding the possibility of another failure. Here we come close to the political implications of what Freud called the "reality principle", the sense that the external world outside ourselves has certain impassable barriers that we need to act within, rather than change. Just as Danny's perceived lack of ability makes him doubt what he's capable of, people who lack confidence in their own abilities will have a very difficult time imagining that their actions can have a meaningful impact on the world. The possibility of political action — strikes, blockades, etc. — becomes slim when the people who could be involved in such things don't believe in their actions having any effect.

We see here how failure is not only a brutal experience when felt at the individual level. Even if it's an unintentional consequence of our cultures of ambition, at the broader social level failure helps perpetuate the status quo by leaving us deskilled and doubtful of our own capacity to act on the world in a way that matters.

"Success"

Not everyone's stories involve the kinds of dramatic narrative failures as the ones described above. But even what we normally consider to be success isn't necessarily all it's cracked up to be.

When ambitious people strive for success, what exactly is it that they want? I outlined in the previous chapter that a major part of ambitious striving involves getting recognition for one's work and having a degree of control and freedom over the work one does. Successful people are inarguably recognised for the work they do. Everyone from small business owners to athletes to artists to CEOs has "made a name for themselves" by having their names forever associated with their work in a way that alienated people's labour isn't recognised to be theirs. But those who find success also find that their success doesn't necessarily make them free — personally, creatively or even economically.

The history of alternative music is replete with musicians discovering and expressing a dissatisfaction towards their own success. A full list would be too massive to compile, but a key example is the song "Bodysnatchers" by Radiohead.[20] The song's lyrics centre on the alienation of being forced into a position against one's will, made to represent and fit into someone else's ideal model rather than follow one's own interests. This is all made evident in a line repeated towards the end of the song: "They got a skin and they put you in." The "skin", the model, is pre-made, but needs a person willing to fit into it and render it operational. When asked to explain the song's meaning, Thom Yorke has cited *The Stepford Wives*, which makes sense given its theme of one's autonomy being stripped away. I think this explanation is likely a diplomatic one, describing the way control can be stripped away without alienating Radiohead's label by criticising them directly. A couple of lines very early in the song, "You killed the sound, removed backbone / A pale imitation with the edges all sawn off", make clear that the song is indeed about the music industry, and that it's Yorke himself whose autonomy has been stripped away by his own accomplishments and those of his band.

In Rainbows, the album on which "Bodysnatchers" appears — and in my opinion, the band's best — was famously one of the first major albums to be sold digitally as a "pay what you want" album. Releasing *In Rainbows* independently was, at the time, a means by which the band could seek an escape from major record labels which might stifle their creativity. "The worst-case scenario", Yorke says in an interview, "would have been: sign another [record] deal, take a load of money, and then you have the machine waiting semi-patiently for you to deliver your product, which they can add to the list of products that make up the myth, la-la-la-la."[21] Selling their album digitally for whatever people were willing to pay for it was a way to evade the restrictions of record deals as Radiohead got more and more successful, getting their music to consumers with no corporate middlemen, and for free. Of course, it turned out that the promise of digital music has pitfalls of its own. More recently, Yorke has been critical not only of major record labels but also of tech platforms like Apple and Google that aim to reduce music to commodifiable "content" rather than artistic expression.[22]

"Bodysnatchers", and the digital rollout of *In Rainbows* more broadly, was the result of Radiohead and Yorke coming to be dissatisfied with their own success, and their dissatisfaction cannot be unique to them. People become artists because they have dreams of being able to create their art free from economic and creative pressures, but that's an impossibility in the world of mainstream music. An album might need to sell hundreds of thousands of copies for record labels to break even on their investments, and this affects what those labels will let bands get away with when they write and record their albums. The lack of creative autonomy expressed in "Bodysnatchers" is the inevitable story of all successful artists.

Artists discovering their lack of creative autonomy in the culture industry is nothing new. If we want a more hard-nosed look at success not being all it's cracked up to be, it behoves us to take a look at the ways in which market competition ensures that even capitalists cannot simply rest on the laurels of their success. In Chapter Two, I discussed the way in which those who don't have bosses — like freelancers, small-business owners or gig-economy hustlers — aren't free from economic coercion. Now it's time to extend that, and explore how capitalists themselves aren't necessarily free from economic coercion.

Capitalists, like everybody, are in some way compelled by the market to make financial decisions which benefit themselves. They might be dealing with much larger sums of money, but they can't spend it wherever they like. Business owners and investors are incentivised to grow whatever business they have a stake in, outcompete direct competitors and make good investments that will generate returns. Personal hang-ups need to be put aside for the more important task of generating steady profits. If a capitalist wants to pay their workers more, or invest in researching and developing alternatives to plastic, or give money to build infrastructure projects in central Africa, they need an economic incentive to do so. And conversely, if they need to pay minimum wage, drive up productivity, or cut costs on worker safety in order to be competitive, then so be it.[23] "Only as a personification of capital", as Marx says in the first volume of *Capital*, "is the capitalist respectable."[24] Capitalists are by no means free to do as they choose with their money. They have to make decisions as if they're nothing but a conduit for reinvesting money.

In *The Communist Manifesto*, decades before the publication of *Capital*, Marx and Engels write that "in bourgeois society capital is independent and has individuality, while the living person is dependent and has no individuality."[25] It's not by mistake that they wrote "*the living person* is dependent", rather than just "the proletariat". They purposefully included the bourgeoisie among those who have no independence in capitalism. Capitalists and workers are both constrained, but their respective economic positions constrain them differently. If we use Foucault's definition of power as "an action upon an action", the market holds a substantial amount of power over the capitalist, because the capitalist needs to grow and outcompete their fellow capitalists if their enterprise is to survive.[26] At the same time, capitalists have power over workers through their ability to fire them. As Søren Mau put it in his recent book, "*proletarians are subjected to capitalists by means of a mechanism of domination which simultaneously subjects everyone to the imperatives of capital*".[27] Capitalists may have the ability to withhold people's payment, which we all need to live, but they're nonetheless cogs in the globe-spanning processes of capital accumulation.

If a capitalist really wants to be free — free from the demands of the market economy, free from being the "personification of capital" and free from constant competition with their fellow capitalists — their only real option is to abandon any goal of reinvestment. This is one of the few reasons why people with more money are actually freer than those who have less; they enter the market to make a profit, while we enter it to make a living.[28] Unlike the rest of us, they really do have the option of taking their money and running, escaping the economy as was described in Chapter Two. If they want, capitalists can buy a modest house or apartment, liquidate their assets and set themselves up with enough funding to receive a certain amount of money every year to live in some degree of material comfort for the rest of their lives. They might spend a little less time hobnobbing in Martha's Vineyard with the Obamas, or lecturing at economic conferences in Europe, but they can rest easy knowing that they no longer need to. But then they cease to be capitalists. Their capital would no longer be reinvested in the economy. To be precise, they would no longer possess capital at all; it would simply be money, which they can hold or spend at will.[29] "The economic character of capitalist becomes firmly fixed to a man only if his money *constantly* functions as capital", and if they give up reinvesting their money, they give up on being a capitalist as well.[30] To actually be autonomous, to realise the idea many have of becoming a capitalist, a capitalist must cease to be a capitalist at all. In this sense — and this sense only — workers and capitalists have a point in common: the true freedom of both classes can only be found in the abolition of their social position. The point here is that even if someone's economic ambitions are realised, and they become successful enough to become a full-fledged capitalist, that doesn't make them as free as is often advertised. They have failed at realising what they actually set out to realise and are left in yet another position of economic coercion.

Failure is practically inevitable in our ambitious societies: either we fail before we accomplish our goals or we experience moments of fleeting success before becoming dissatisfied; before becoming aware of how, despite all our successes, we're still limited by broader economic forces.

Ambition's gravediggers

I've painted a pretty bleak picture in the two sections above. Ambition creates two kinds of failures. The first are outright failures, blocked from achieving their goals at all. The second are those who come to realise they've won pyrrhic victories and lost the autonomy they thought they'd have to the profit motive, a failure in its own right. Where is there to go after mapping an ambitious society of "depressives and losers"? What potential can be found in endemic failure?

There's a lot of discourse in the white-collar world about the value of failure as an opportunity. Corporate advice abounds on how failure is an opportunity to learn, to reassess, to explore, to pause and to gain insights that couldn't have been gathered by coasting one's way to success.[31] In these contexts, success remains the primary mode of action, and failure only exists as a detour on the path of success.[32] A common job interview question I've received has been about how I've overcome obstacles or setbacks, which is a euphemistic way of asking how I've spun initial failures into success — and learned the value of "perseverance" and "goal-oriented thinking" and all that professional lingo. I don't want to repeat the tired business-school mantra that failing is an opportunity to pick yourself up, dust yourself off and start again, because I think that kind of advice wallpapers over structural challenges and promotes the sham of individual struggles for success. But I do think failure is an opportunity, if for something else entirely.

In the previous chapter I mentioned that Foucault saw subjectivation as a process of subjugation. To become a certain kind of subject involves an allegiance to one's subjectivity, to be subject to oneself, in the same manner as one would understand terms like "royal subjects" or "religious subjects". Now is the time to discuss the reversal or destruction of that process, of *de*subjectivation. Desubjectivation is not simply the construction of oneself, or even the self-creation of a new self — for who would be doing the creating? Rather, desubjectivation "entails a radically different conception: freedom, not just from others, but from oneself, or even from being anything like a *self* or entity of any sort".[33] The freedom of throwing away the fixed ideas one has not only of their goals, but of themselves as able or wanting to accomplish those goals. This isn't the freedom imagined by right-wing Nietzscheans who imagine the *Übermensch* as an entrepreneur, or by "Lean-In feminists" who promote themselves as icons of feminism while subjugating any women working for them. This is a freedom which can be found not by discovering nor constructing nor improving what we are, but by following Foucault's advice and refusing what we are.[34]

One can't just decide to be something other than oneself; it's not a decision one can casually make, like we're window-shopping for identities. As Freud wrote, "People never willingly abandon a libidinal position".[35] Rather, "Calling the subject into question means that one would have to experience something leading to its actual destruction, its decomposition, its explosion, its conversion into something else."[36] Examples can be found in the many initiation rituals around the world centred upon pain: scarification, circumcision, teeth sharpening, etc. We can understand these ritual initiations as ceremonies of de- (and then re-)subjectivation, as pain is a totalising experience through which an initiate can think of absolutely nothing else, and their actual experience of the pain can't be shared with the people around them.[37] Pain works to strip the initiate of their subjectivity, so they can be established as an adult by the ceremony's conclusion.[38] The sting of failure might not be as dramatic as these initiation ceremonies, but it's nonetheless a totalising experience to the person involved. Failure — either the catastrophic kind or the kind when the subject comes to realise their life's work isn't what was promised to them — strips a person of all the things they used to identify themselves: their goals, their life's teleology, all the investments they've made in their human capital, oftentimes their actual money. Suddenly it's all meaningless. Once someone has failed to live up to society's expectations of them and their own expectations of themselves, all they're left with is shame, guilt and humiliation. There's a good chance that someone could emerge from that experience being changed in a fundamental way.

But what have they changed into? Not much, but that doesn't mean people aren't capable of collective action in their socially maligned position. The Iranian-American sociologist Asef Bayat uses the term "nonmovement" to refer to the kinds of collective action undertaken out of desperation rather than an allegiance to a political ideology or to one's supposed revolutionary potential. Nonmovements are "the collective actions of noncollective actors", individual acts of rebellion that often snowball into something greater than the sum of their parts.[39] Rather than a steadfast allegiance to a political party, or an ideological position or a coherent goal, nonmovements' power to affect society comes from "the power of big numbers".[40] A single person torching a car, throwing a brick through a window, or fighting a cop is a lone actor, and will be commented upon by the media as an untreated mental health case at best and a racialised terrorist at worst. But what happens when you have hundreds of people engaging in these actions? It doesn't matter if they share a political ideology or a cultural background, or if they know each other in any way. It's a riot, and *that* has a political impact, whether the people in the riot recognise it or not.

Nonmovements are the movements engaged in by a class of failures. But how can failures be understood as a class? The historian EP Thompson wrote that "class happens when some men, as a result of common experiences (inherited or shared), feel and articulate the identity of their interests as between themselves, and as against other men whose interests are different from (and usually opposed to) theirs".[41] Put simply, a class comes to exist when its members realise their similarity, and the similarity of their interests, which are in conflict with the interests of other classes. In this way, we could speak of a class of failures, who recognise themselves and people like them as failures and who share each other's interests.

What interests do failures have? Failures are those who have been unable to achieve their goals and desires and have lost their interest and investment in the supposed benefits of the capitalist economy. If they remain attached to these goals through their failure, they become resentful, as Danny does in *Barracuda*. But if they discard their attachments to their goals and their life's telos, if they reclaim self-ownership by abandoning their goals as Stirner suggests, they disinvest from the capitalist economy and become capitalism's "gravediggers", as Marx and Engels write in *The Communist Manifesto*.[42] When Marx and Engels wrote that all the proletariat has to lose is their chains, what they meant was that unlike every other class, the proletariat quite literally has nothing invested in the capitalist economy. It owns no stocks, no rental properties, no land, no machines and no factories.[43] This class of downwardly mobile failures are, or can be, in the same position. When someone fails, they're presented with a choice: to reinvest in the economy and themselves, pick themselves up and try again; or to disinvest further, understand the precarity of their own position and become revolutionary.

This is how neoliberal society produces a class of its own gravediggers. Once our ambitious hopes have been tarnished by the restrictions of capital, once we've sacrificed everything in a quixotic struggle for goals that we've failed to actualise, once we've dropped out, burned out and given up, what is to be done? In class struggle, the target is always the ruling class, yes. But if it's our subjectivity which brings us to an immiserated social position, then by abandoning that subjectivity we turn into the class ready to put a stop not only to work but to the subjective structure which makes us *desire* work. When an aim or purpose has defined someone's entire life, and they no longer have it, that can be felt as a deeply traumatic experience, as if something which made you who you are has been taken from you. But we should follow Max Stirner's advice from earlier in this chapter, and not fight to be possessed by our fixed ideas of who we're supposed to be. It's only by throwing away these fixed ideas, our ambitions, that we can truly be free.

5. Radical Ambitions?

"Be moderate", the trimmers cry,
Who dread the tyrants' thunder.
"You ask too much and people fly
From you aghast in wonder."
'Tis passing strange, for I declare
Such statements give me mirth,
For our demands most moderate are,
We only want the earth.
— James Connolly, "We Only Want the Earth"[1]

The last thing I should promise would be to "improve" mankind.
No new idols are erected by me; let the old ones learn what feet
of clay mean. Overthrowing idols (my word for "ideals")—that
comes closer to being part of my craft.
— Friedrich Nietzsche, *Ecce Homo*[2]

At least since Montaigne wrote that "for ambition's sake, let us reject ambition", we've been aware that any attempt to get rid of ambition seemingly contains an element of paradox.[3] If we've learned anything so far, it's that ambition needs certain conditions to exist if it's going to emerge and proliferate — a society made up of different classes; the theoretical possibility of social mobility between those classes; lives to be seen as investment strategies a la human capital theory; a lack which people feel the need to overcome through personal glory and material acquisition; etc. — and any movement to abolish ambition means we'd need to abolish these conditions as well. So, any attempt to eliminate ambition would require changing the world in a dramatic way, ending class society at the very least. But how can we desire to change the world without being ambitious ourselves? Well, our ambition to change the world might be a *kind* of ambition, certainly, but it's an ambition which falls so far outside of the ambitious paradigm cultivated by neoliberal culture that it loses all resemblance. It's an ambition for destruction, or escape, and it's an ambition that isn't attached to an ideal or a model of the future. The "ambition to abolish ambition", as we might call it, and the more mundane social, economic and political ambitions this book has criticised thus far are very different indeed.

Two kinds of power

It might be useful to tease out this distinction by drawing on the French political thinker Georges Sorel and his own distinction not between two kinds of ambition, but two kinds of political violence. In his book *Reflections on Violence*, Sorel argues that the violence done by the state ("bourgeois force") and that committed in resistance to or against the state ("proletarian violence") are different based on who they are enacted by and what they achieve. Through institutions like the police and the military, bourgeois force serves to secure comfortable peace, the continuation of the status quo. Because it serves the status quo, Sorel thought that by its very nature bourgeois force is incapable of creating anything new, and that in fact it *prevents* newness from emerging. What Sorel calls proletarian violence, on the other hand, serves to upend the social order, because by engaging in class struggle, it jumpstarts the engine of social-historical change. It can stimulate the emergence of new social forms, for instance when capitalism emerged in response to the class struggles of feudal Europe. Early in their careers, Marx and Engels famously wrote that all history "is the history of class struggle", so to give up on (violent) class struggle is, for Sorel, to give up on the possibility of social change and history itself.

In Sorel's day, a century ago, and in our own times as well, this understanding of violence is a fairly radical departure from the political norm. Then as much as now, violence was seen as a strictly negative phenomenon, and the idea that we should avoid using violence to achieve political ends was pushed into public discourse even by supposedly radical academic sociologists, journalists and politicians, all of whom Sorel saw as his chief adversaries. According to this consensus, we "civilised" societies have progressed beyond the necessity of violence, and we have more acceptable means of political activity. But it isn't true that we've progressed beyond violence, because the state uses it to achieve its ends constantly. When a renter needs to be evicted by force, the police are there to do so. When workers occupy a factory, the police are ready to sort them out. When a country in the Middle East isn't amenable to trading its oil to the United States for a low enough price and refuses to budge, military violence is a strong negotiating tool. An absence of violence isn't necessarily indicative of a movement from barbarism to civilisation, Sorel writes. Instead, the reduction of violence indicates the victory of bourgeois force and the drowning of revolutionary violence "in the saliva of professors".[4]

Sorel's insistence on (proletarian) violence having a creative, aesthetic function is one of the reasons why he remains a relatively controversial and lesser-known thinker to this day, especially in the socialist tradition. In fact, when

I first came across Sorel in the mid- to late 2010s, his absence from the then popular discourse on "accelerationism" was surprising. The notion propagated by vulgar accelerationists that the only way to meaningfully change the social order is to usher in the total collapse of society seems to resonate with Sorel's assertion that comfortable social peace must be destroyed through aesthetic acts of revolutionary violence. Though he was an anarchist, Sorel was eventually picked up as an influence on Mussolini and became an important intellectual inspiration for fascist violence. But Sorel's influence isn't limited purely to fascists.

Walter Benjamin, in his essay "Critique of Violence", expands upon Sorel's distinction between two kinds of violence, in a way that is perhaps more anarchistic than the self-proclaimed anarchism of the latter.[5] Whereas the dividing line between the two kinds of violence for Sorel hinges upon their source and function,[6] Benjamin's distinction hinges upon violence and its relationship to law: the first kind of violence is either "lawmaking" or "law-preserving", and works to instate a new legal order, or reinforce the law as it currently exists; the second kind of violence is "law destroying", and seeks to eliminate law without founding a new legal system.[7] As Benjamin says, "If the former sets boundaries, the latter boundlessly destroys them".[8]

To illustrate his point, Benjamin borrows a comparison from Sorel: that between the *political* general strike and the *proletarian* general strike. The former is essentially an act of political and economic blackmail, threatening politicians and capitalists with continued work stoppages until certain legal demands are met. The demands might well be valuable — more pay, less hours, better benefits — but "the strengthening of state power is the basis of their conceptions", whether it be the same state power or an updated one with a few more parliamentarians from the working class.[9] The proletarian general strike, as Benjamin writes, "takes place not in readiness to resume work following external concessions and this or that modification to working conditions, but in the determination to resume only *a wholly transformed work*, no longer enforced by the state".[10] The first kind of general strike is itching to go back to work once its conditions are met, but the second refuses to accept any conditions at all. Work will only resume for those in the latter category once their refusal of work starts having an appreciable effect on how society operates, once the flow of commodities and money breaks down and something else can emerge. Those who know their twentieth-century history would be correct to see a resemblance to France's abortive May '68 revolution in this distinction. Where the majority of the French Communist Party and the trade unions wanted a return to work once they got higher salaries and benefits, the students and the more radical strikers wanted the stoppages to continue indefinitely.

The philosopher Oxana Timofeeva provides an example from recent Russian history which shows "a clear confrontation" between Benjamin's two kinds of violence.[11] In 2018, a group of sisters in their late teens banded together to attack and kill their incredibly abusive father. In this story, the father is a kind of representative of law-preserving violence. He was well-connected with the local police, and domestic violence isn't a criminal offense in Russia, so there was no legal recourse his daughters could take against him. After they killed him, the legal system sided entirely with their murdered father, and the girls were sent to jail for between eight and twenty years. The (patriarchal) law-preserving violence of their father's abuse mirrors the law-preserving violence of the police and state, which in the end supported him entirely. On the other hand, the group of daughters are representatives of law-destroying violence. They had no legal system defending their actions, and they murdered their father for no other reason than to free themselves from more years of his abuse. This is why Benjamin ends his essay with the proclamation that law-destroying violence may also be called "sovereign violence", because it acts for itself, and there is nothing outside it that matters.[12] It has no legal defence and no other motive besides affirming its own capacity.

The Italian philosopher Giorgio Agamben picks up where Sorel and Benjamin left off, making his distinction not between two kinds of violence and their relationship to the law, but between two forms of power: *pouvoir constituant* and *puissance destituante*, which translate roughly to "constituent power" and "destituent potential", respectively. Agamben cites Benjamin directly in his writing on this topic, so it's no coincidence that Agamben's categories of power roughly correspond to Benjamin's categories of violence. "While a constituent power destroys law only to recreate it in a new form", Agamben writes, "destituent power, in so far as it *deposes once and for all the law*, can open a really new historical epoch".[13] What began as Benjamin's "law-preserving", "law-making" and "law-destroying" violence here become "constituted power", "constituent power" and "destituent power". Much like Benjamin, Agamben's preference is for the latter category.

Agamben's concept is a novel one, and what destituent power looks like in practice is often unclear. But all this might make a little more sense once we unpack the meaning of the word "destitute" as a verb. English speakers like myself are most familiar with the word as an adjective, usually meaning something like "poor" or "indigent", describing those on the lowest rung of the social hierarchy. The adjective form of "destitute" approaches Agamben's usage when it comes to mean "deprived" or "abandoned", because these words imply a subject responsible for making someone destitute. Someone can only be abandoned, made destitute, *by someone*. The Latin verb *destituere*, meaning "to abandon; put aside, let drop, knock down",[14] recalls this second meaning, but from the perspective of the subject abandoning something, making something destitute by abandoning it or by "letting it drop". This is the meaning Agamben draws from in his coinage of "destituent potential": the capacity or potential to perpetually abandon or escape institutions of power, and to thereby bring about their demise.

For a specific example, let's turn to the anonymous French group the Invisible Committee, and their writings on the subject. Certainly more direct than Agamben, they write that to destitute something "is to deprive it of its foundation".[15] In the same way that people at the margins of society are described as "destitute" when they lack the means to survive at the most basic level, to destitute institutions is to eliminate their conditions and to draw away their sources of support, to deprive the institutions of what *they* need to survive. Take the university, for example. As the Invisible Committee write:

> To destitute the university is to establish, at a distance, the places of research, of education and thought, that are more vibrant and demanding than it is — which would not be hard — and to greet the arrival of the last vigorous minds who are tired of frequenting the academic zombies, and only then to administer its death blow.[16]

To render the university destitute is not to fix the current university system, nor is it to adopt the current right-wing culture war stratagem of starting an "anti-woke" scam and calling it a university.[17] It's to abandon the university and the institutionalised form higher education has taken.[18]

Unlike constituent power, which opposes institutions by either attacking them directly or forming parallel institutions of its own, destituent potential isn't interested in opposing anything. Rather than direct attack, it forces its targets into a position where fighting is no longer economical. To use an analogy to military strategy, the relationship between constituent power and the status quo is most similar to the fighting which took place during World War I: two symmetrical powers, both of which were literally entrenched in position, fighting to take slivers of each other's territories while endlessly maintaining their forces. The fighting is slow and cumbersome, and what little gains are made come at what is often a large price. On the other hand, we can compare destituent potential to the tactics of guerrilla warfare, where the objective is most often to wear down a much more powerful enemy through constant escapes, rather than to compete with force.[19] During the Arab Revolt described by T.E. Lawrence, the Ottoman Empire held massive amounts of land in the Levant — 140,000 square miles by Lawrence's estimation — but stretching their forces thin made them vulnerable, and the Arabs Lawrence joined weren't strong enough to fight the Turks head on; to wade into explicit battle against them would have been suicide. Instead, the Arab guerrillas hit not the Turks' heads but their wallets. "The Arabs had nothing material to lose, so they were to defend nothing and to shoot nothing", Lawrence writes.[20] Their real targets were the Turks' railways and supply lines, rather than men with guns who could shoot back. Dispersal over a massive range and "never engaging the enemy at all" were the winning strategies.[21] When the Invisible Committee declares that "the finest destituent victories are often those where the battle simply never takes place", one cannot help but make the comparison with guerrilla warfare's strategic avoidance of direct confrontation.[22]

To put it simply: where constituent power seeks to wield authority to depose an institution and reinstate a new one, destituent potential wears down whatever existing power it can while refusing to take power for itself.

The only radical ambitions are destituent ambitions

The theory of destituent potential allows us to find a way out of the paradox with which I opened this chapter. All the ambitions we see today don't want to challenge the foundations of the economy, nor get rid of ambition and its grasp on people's conceptions of themselves. Successful people are, of course, beneficiaries of the economy and the reign of ambition, so why on earth would they want to see such a situation changed? The ambition described in this chapter is nothing like that at all. In fact the ambition to abolish, overcome or abandon ambition itself can be called a "destituent ambition", in the sense that, to paraphrase the Invisible Committee, it's an ambitious task to deprive ambition of its very foundations.

This is why, if we want to tackle ambition as a central affect in neoliberal societies, simply getting rid of individual ambitious people is never going to be a sufficient solution. There are thousands, if not millions, of Donald Trumps, Joe Bidens, Rishi Sunaks and Elon Musks chomping at the bit for a chance to grasp whatever power they can get their hands on. Replacing an ambitious person currently in power doesn't change any of the conditions which brought them to power in the first place and allowed their ambitions to thrive. While criticising ambition as much as his contemporaries, Francis Bacon was nonetheless correct when he wrote that replacing one ambitious person with another was one of the ways in which ambition could be useful to the ruling class. "There is use also of ambitious men", Bacon writes in his essay "On Ambition", "in pulling down the greatness of any subject that overtops; as Tiberius used Macro, in the pulling down of Sejanus."[23] In other words, if those in power sense that someone is getting too big for their britches and their ambitions risk disrupting the social order in an unacceptable way, other ambitious people can be manipulated to replace them.

The specific episode of Roman history which Bacon draws from is an instructive case. He's referring to the execution of the Roman Praetorian guard commander Lucius Aelius Sejanus in 31 AD and his quick replacement by Naevius Sutorius Macro. The emperor Tiberius had left the management of Rome to Sejanus since 26 AD, and Sejanus had been steadily accumulating power, as was fairly common among potentially traitorous Roman soldiers around that time. According to the version of the story Bacon is drawing from,[24] Tiberius was becoming suspicious of Sejanus, who was consolidating his power and at risk of becoming a threat, so Tiberius exploited Macro's own political ambitions by encouraging him to oust Sejanus and replace him. Fittingly, Macro ended up helping Caligula rise to power following Tiberius's death, and when Macro's rise suddenly became a threat to Caligula, the latter arrested Macro, stripped him of his office and title and eventually drove him to suicide.

The story of Sejanus, Tiberius, Macro and Caligula shows the futility of getting rid of ambitious individuals without altering the structure of power. If one replaces an ambitious person with another, they'll continue to replace each other ad infinitum while the social order moves along unhindered and unchanged. This is all well and good if one has faith in the social order as it currently stands — liberal democracy, the rule of law, capitalism, etc. — but for those of us who don't, who recognise the necessity of revolutionary change, Sejanus's replacement with Macro and Tiberius's replacement with Caligula demonstrate the futility of reformism, and the impossibility of ambitious individuals making a difference to a system many times older and more powerful than they are. Keep in mind, Francis Bacon was no revolutionary, and he certainly wasn't writing on behalf of the European poor. He frames "On Ambition" as an offer of advice to the nobility of his day about how ambition is beneficial or harmful to the social order, and he used the replacement of Sejanus with Macro as an example of how ambition can be used to maintain the social order rather than tear it asunder.

So many stories of electoral politics, even supposedly radical politics, recall Macro replacing Sejanus and Caligula replacing Tiberius. On the left, we've become all too familiar with political hopefuls, driven by an ambition to change the world once they enter the halls of power, who enter parliaments, congresses and governments only to find themselves changed in the process.

In the US there are any number of politicians who, after an initial success on a "radical" platform, become subsumed into the politics of the Democratic Party and more concerned about the longevity of their own political careers than with changing anything. Alexandria Ocasio-Cortez is one of recent note. Ocasio-Cortez initially made a name for herself as a different kind of politician inside the US's Democratic Party, with her pre-political background featuring work as a bartender rather than as a consultant or a lawyer, making claims like "In any other country [she and Joe Biden] would not be in the same party".[25] With statements like these, Ocasio-Cortez rhetorically separates herself from the Democratic Party's more centrist elements like Joe Biden and Nancy Pelosi.

One can make a good assessment of "AOC's" political transformation by comparing her statements around 2018, during her optimistic congressional campaign and the period after her election, to her statements, actions and votes in the years since. In 2018 she was willing to call Israel's domination of Palestine an "occupation", but quickly backflipped when pushed, stressing Israel's "right to exist" and her commitment to the two-state solution, and downplaying the Israeli occupation as something only occurring in West Bank settlements.[26] But at least she was willing to openly criticise Israel's human rights abuses on the campaign trail, implying that she should put some political power that way when elected. In 2021, however, when it came time to vote on whether Israel should receive even more funding for its "defence", Ocasio-Cortez cried in Congress and voted "present", rather than a definitive yes or no.[27] Even her stated commitments to workers and "democratic socialism" were abandoned in time. When a train derailment in Ohio became a public health crisis and a national scandal, Ocasio-Cortez publicly criticised the freight companies for their shoddy working conditions and the unsafe practices which led to the derailment. But when push came to shove, and it came time to vote on whether those same rail workers were allowed to go on strike to improve their working conditions, she voted to prevent the workers from striking.[28] She even claimed that doing so was supported by the majority of rank-and-file union members in the rail sector, which was far from the truth.

One of Ocasio-Cortez's more egregious acts was in 2021, when she attended the illustrious Met Gala fashion event — for which a single ticket cost $35,000 — in a white dress emblazoned with the phrase "Tax the rich".[29] A lot of ink has been spilled defending Ocasio-Cortez and her dress, usually with claims like, "She's raising awareness" for such and such a cause, and that we would see the impact in time. But writing this nearly three years later, with the incident well and truly behind us, what can we say did wearing the dress actually accomplish? Did it indeed lead to higher taxes on the US's wealthiest? Did it abolish the US Immigration and Customs Enforcement agency and put an end to their horrific reign over the USA's southern border? Certainly not. But Ocasio-Cortez's dress succeeded in one thing: it raised her political profile as a "radical" politician without damaging her career ambitions. To go to the Met Gala in a bog-standard expensive dress would not have constituted the kind of symbolic gesture Ocasio-Cortez has made part and parcel of her congressional tenure, and to actually protest the event in any substantive way would have made her the enemy of New York high society and potentially impacted any future campaigns for the senate or presidency. So she picked the middle ground: a symbolic gesture, a kernel of a protest that puts nothing on the line. As a critic of hers writes, "It's one thing to go to the [Met Gala]; it's another to blare out a message that you disapprove of the party while you're there."[30] The whole incident reminds one a little too much of a high school student attending a party that they insist they're too cool to attend.

The parliamentary strategies of Ocasio-Cortez are indicative of the failure of electoralism and mainstream political ambitions, but they aren't the main target of destitution's critique of constituent power. Leninism, and its strategy of reappropriating capitalist institutions, *is* such a target, the steel that sharpens destitution's sword. Returning to Benjamin's vocabulary from earlier, the October revolution of 1917 is the exemplar of law-making violence — and constituent power — since it deposed the old legal system, the absolute monarchy of the tsars, to instate a totally new one based on state socialism. Quite literally, it sought to create a new constitution.

But the constituent power of Leninism depended upon taking hold of institutions that had developed under capitalism and using them to supposedly develop socialism. The Leninist attitude towards state power shows this to be a mistake. The Leninist theory of the state argues that the state began as a mediator of hostile class relationships. The main thing stopping the working class from revolting, so the theory goes, is that any revolution would be put down by the state. Therefore the state exists as a representative and a defender of the ruling class, in that it defends the ruling classes' interests, but it purports to represent the interests of all society. From the theory, it follows that once classes are abolished, there won't be any class antagonism, so the state will "wither away" in time, since it'll no longer be useful.[31] The Leninist theory of the state argues that socialists should take hold of state power and use it to develop communism, because once communism has been achieved, state power will eventually disappear.

But Lenin was mistaken in thinking that the state won't outlive its usefulness. No matter how or why something is set up, it won't necessarily disappear of its own accord or abolish itself because it isn't necessary anymore.[32] The existence of human appendices and ostrich wings shows that something can stick around long after it's no longer functionally useful. For, what is the state exactly? At the macroscopic level the state is notoriously difficult to define, but at the microscopic level it's composed of cops, officials, bureaucrats, surveyors, regulators and so many other professionals, all of whom have salaries and positions of authority they'll be willing to defend. Developing a class of "professional revolutionaries" whose income is supported by party funds turns the task of revolutionary activity into a profession, like any other.[33] Even if their job does become useless, it'd take a lot of convincing for a bureaucrat to voluntarily abolish their own job and work in a factory. Even today there are a large amount of "bullshit jobs" about which even the people who work these jobs know that they don't need to exist.[34] Leninism's theory of the state and its disappearance might have been theoretically sound in the abstract, but it doesn't translate to a world of individual people with their own material interests. Leninism's errors regarding the "withering away" of the state are replicated in Lenin's writing on Taylorism, the "scientific management" of workers.

Lenin recognised Taylorism as a brutal practice of worker exploitation, but like his theory of the state, he argued that Taylorism could be reappropriated for socialist purposes. By studying workers' movements and finding the most optimal way for them to do their jobs, Lenin wrote, "the capitalist obtains an enormous profit, but the workers toil four times as hard."[35] This means an individual worker could be paid more, even double their previous wage, but the capitalist would still be the one raking in the lion's share of the profits. Using Taylorism and its idea of the optimal worker's performance, capitalists can profitably sack most of their workers and keep only those who fall close to the "model" worker. But even in saying all this, Lenin wasn't anti-Taylorist. Rather, he thought that Taylorism was an efficient practice within capitalist manufacturing, but the irrationality and chaos capitalism's profit-driven distribution was based on was the real problem:

> What a vast amount of labour is wasted at present owing to the disorganised and chaotic character of capitalist production as a whole! How much time is wasted as the raw materials pass to the factory through the hands of hundreds of buyers and middlemen, while the requirements of the market are unknown! [...] The Taylor system — without its initiators knowing or wishing it — is preparing the time when the proletariat will take over all social production and appoint its own workers' committees for the purpose of properly distributing and rationalising all social labour. Large-scale production, machinery, railways, telephone — all provide thousands of opportunities to cut by three-fourths the working time of the organised workers and make them four times better off than they are today.[36]

There will come a time when the Taylorism developed under capitalism will be replaced by the People's Taylorism. Employee's movements will continue to be modelled and tracked to find the most efficient labour process, but it'll all be in service of some nebulous time in the future when we can theoretically work less, no doubt giving us more time to attend "workers' committees". This was written more than a century ago, but the sentiment still holds true. We're surrounded today by so many institutions and ways of living that no one would ever wish to take over or even leave standing. "Who would wish to reappropriate nuclear power plants, Amazon's warehouses, the expressways, ad agencies", and so much else?[37]

The disappointing outcomes of constituted and constituent power, parliamentary social democracy and revolutionary socialism, indicate that the common ambition of politics — to take hold of institutional power and then change the world — is not as effective as we might hope. It's not the people managing the institutions, but the institutions themselves that should be gotten rid of and replaced with nothing. It's not for nothing that the rallying cry of the "destituent insurrection" in Argentina in 2001 was "¡Que se vayan todos!" — "They all must go!", in English.[38] As succinctly as possible, the chant declares that power itself must neither be taken nor allowed to continue existing unhindered. And nothing can be allowed to remain; it must *all* go. And as for those with political ambitions, who would use their power to reinforce old laws or create new ones, the parliamentarians and professional revolutionaries, they must all go too.

An aimless communism

In the first chapter of this book, I brought up the fact that ambition is usually regarded to be good or bad based on what it's aimed towards. Good ambitions are usually things like career success, while things like status and political power are categorised as bad ambitions. While I don't make this distinction, I still agree that the presence of directionality is ambition's salient characteristic. Ambition isn't really ambition at all unless it's an ambition *for something*: an object, a purpose, a goal, a telos. Therefore, finally overcoming, abandoning or destituting ambition requires that we also give up on the idea of an overarching telos which defines both the world and our actions within it.

Abandoning the idea of telos is an admittedly difficult task for a communist. Communism has long been associated with a teleological interpretation of history and class struggle. Marx deserves at least some of the blame for this, since his portrayal of history as a linear development from the earliest stages of "primitive communism" (more on that in the next chapter) to slave societies, feudalism and eventually capitalism presents communism as the end point of human history, in the sense of "end" as both completion and purpose. He phrased it thusly in his *1844 Manuscripts*: "Communism is the riddle of history solved, and it knows itself to be this solution."[39] Marx echoes a similarly teleological understanding of history nearly a decade later, towards the end of an essay on British colonialism in India. He concludes the essay by commenting upon the untold brutality meted out to the people of India, carried out "only by the vilest interests" of the English colonists.[40] But he asks rhetorically whether all this bloodshed may have been the result of England acting as "the unconscious tool of history" by hurrying the Indian subcontinent along the path of civilisation and productive activity, like a student skipping a year at school.[41] The implication is that since capitalism and then communism are the destiny of human societies, India's colonisation was an unfortunate necessity of world-historical capital-P Progress. That communism is supposedly the ultimate aim of history, and that the development of capitalism can be seen as positive because it leads closer to communism, is by necessity a teleological claim.

But an important aspect is missing in this analysis: the question of *what communism is*. The diagnosis of Marx's communism as a teleological concept only really makes sense if communism is imagined as a system of economic activity in the same way that feudalism and capitalism are. Some of the most important communist writings, including Marx's own, emphasise the opposite: that communism is a process rather than a thing. In *The German Ideology*, for example, Marx and Engels give their famous definition that communism is "the *real* movement which abolishes the present state of things".[42] Engels, in a lesser-known early text, "The Principles of Communism", echoes this processual earlier definition, writing that communism is at once "the condition for the liberation of the proletariat" and the abolition of private property.[43] Later in Marx's life, towards the end of the first volume of *Capital*, he borrows from Hegel in writing that the end of capitalism will be the "the negation of [capitalism's] negation, the expropriation of the expropriators".[44] That these examples use words which end with the -tion suffix (negation, liberation, expropriation, abolition) is not an insignificant detail. It stresses the difference between a world where class society is abolished, *a thing*, and the abolition of class society, *a process*. Some will argue that, sure, Marx and Engels do write that a communist society will be one in which it's possible for someone to "hunt in the morning, fish in the afternoon, rear cattle in the evening, [and] criticise after dinner" without ever being tied to any of those positions as one would be in a traditional job.[45] But this is more in the spirit of what they mean by "abolishing the present state of things", since they use this as an example of a society which has abolished — or destituted, if you like — the division of labour and the subjectivisation of oneself as a "hunter, fisherman, herdsman or critic" which comes along with it.[46] Marx's writings on communism, from his earliest to his latest, describe communism as a process rather than an ideal, a plan or a complete economic system.

Following this absence of a description of a communist society in Marx's writing, the most compelling descriptions of communism in recent times are those which similarly emphasise the process of communism, occasionally called "communisation" to stress the -tion suffix I mentioned above.[47] For example, there's the Invisible Committee again, who define communism as "the uncovering of what is common *and* the building of a force [...], the matrix of a meticulous, audacious assault on domination."[48] To others, communism is "the assortment of social practices leading to the transformation of consciousness and reality on every level".[49] In his wonderful recent book on destituent communism, Marcello Tarì draws on Marx and Engels's definition when outlining his ideas, writing that "by communism, we mean the real movement that *destitutes* the present state of things."[50] None of these quotes spell out what a communist society will look like, and all involved are rightfully suspicious of those who do.[51] Examples abound of communism not being described as a *thing*, or an image, or a kind of society. It is, above all, a movement, a process of abolition, overcoming and destitution without a model directing or motivating it.

Communism is similar to destitution in this regard, as they both reject "realisation" as an overarching political principle. They each refuse "the idea that political action consists in realizing, in facts or deeds, a doctrine, a philosophy, an ideal, a plan".[52] This puts them in stark opposition to practically the entire history of political thought in the West. Political campaigns themselves operate on the principle of realisation. If we all band together to vote in so-and-so, they'll put their heads together and figure out a way to make their political ideas and programs into a reality. And this is equally true whether those ideas are an improvement or not, whether the plan on offer is a $15 minimum wage in the US or the UK deciding to ship refugees to offshore detention centres in Rwanda. The history of pre-Marxist socialism especially is full of utopians named not because of their fanciful ideas (one of which was turning oceans into lemonade), but because their models and plans for perfectly functioning socialist societies were made without consideration for the class struggles of their time. Just as Thomas More sketched out *Utopia*, utopian socialists like Charles Fourier and Henri de Saint-Simon drew up their plans for a perfect society and implored the people of the world to realise their complete vision.

Realisation is such a dominant principle in political thought that one looks a bit ridiculous without it. Traditional (constituent) political thinkers who have plans or models for a new political order drawn up tend to argue that a focus on destitution and destituent potential is an admission of failure, but I think this is the wrong way of looking at the issue. We shouldn't let an *unwillingness* to take power or draw up plans be mistaken for an *inability* to do so. Marcello Tarì cites an Italian philosopher's response to various uprisings in Europe: "Instead of a constituent power, today's uprisings recall a destituent power — capable of undermining the previous order but unable to create a new one."[53] The mistake that this philosopher and those like him make is assuming that if those involved in an uprising aren't interested in creating a new social order, it confirms that they're unable to do so. Arguments such as these are why Tarì asserts that the relationship between constituent and destituent politics isn't simply one of parallel opposition, but is rather a complete non-relationship. "They neither begin from the same premises nor do they aim for the same kind of conclusion."[54] The premise of constituent politics is that all political action must necessarily be in service of the creation of a new order of things, the realisation of a political goal or model. The premise of destituent politics is the abandonment and destruction of the current order and the refusal to plan or create or realise a new order of things. Again, this is a premise destitution shares with communism. Neither has an aim nor a model they seek to realise in the world. Both are processes that wish to erode the present state of things.

Which brings me again to the question at the heart of this chapter. Can communism — particularly a destituent communism — still be described as ambitious? If Chantal Jaquet is correct in saying that "the precondition for any ambition is the representation of a real or imaginary model that the individual desires to realize", it seems as though an aimless, destituent communism can't really be described as "ambitious" at all.[55] As I said above, ambition is defined by its aim and its directionality. Ambition is an ambition *for* something or *to* something. To be properly described as ambitious, our desires have to be channelled in certain directions through images of the future. An ambitious child imagines themselves to be president in the future, or a CEO. They can't be called ambitious without having a sense of their future potential which they're then driven to realise through their actions. This understanding of ambition is a world apart from destituent communism as I've described it here. Revolutionary politics is often described as "ambitious" as a pejorative by those who wish to see it fail, but if we use the same definition of ambition as has been used throughout this book, as the teleologisation of desire towards an imagined end, communism in the truly Marxist and destituent sense isn't ambitious at all. It offers no utopian visions of the future, no ideals or images to which everybody's will should be bent. There is nothing to realise in communism besides our own capacity to fight. Ambition is defined by what it's aiming towards, but any communism worthy of the name is nothing more — and nothing less — than an aimless process.

6. The World Against Ambition

When I was the stream, when I was the
forest, when I was still the field
when I was every hoof, foot,
fin and wing, when I
was the sky itself,

no one ever asked me did I have a purpose, no one ever
wondered was there anything I might need,
for there was nothing
I could not love.

— Meister Eckhart, "When I Was the Forest"

The whole character of a species—its species character—is
contained in the character of its life-activity; and free, conscious
activity is man's species character. Life itself appears only as a
means to life.

— Karl Marx, "Economic and Philosophic
Manuscripts of 1844"[1]

Women's (lack of) ambition

If we're to explore what a world without ambition might look like, I'd be remiss in ignoring a large section of the population who already live non-ambitious lives and what follows.

Women, for a number of reasons, are generally less ambitious than men. This is, in part, due to the very real backlash towards women in leadership positions around the world, since misogynists consider women to be "too emotional" to lead effectively, or to be trusted atop a workplace hierarchy. Another explanation given for women's lack of ambition is that the sacrifices women must make for the sake of their ambitions are more significant than those made by men.[2] In a traditional heterosexual marriage, if a woman wants children, she'll need to take a substantial amount of time off due to her pregnancy. And in a world where women continue to do most of the domestic labour,[3] the presence of children and a husband leads to a disproportionate increase of unpaid labour done by women inside the home. These are sacrifices men, generally, don't have to make, as it's far more acceptable for men to work all the way through their spouse's pregnancy, and thus they are left with more time to advance their careers. Lastly, because of the previous examples, ambitious men who seek power and status are generally seen in a positive light, as assertive people who know what they want, while ambitious women who seek the same are perceived as greedy and irrational.

An explanation for this, beyond the reasons given in popular liberal-feminist circles, is that the same historical and economic operations which made men ambitious simply weren't directed towards women. Earlier in this book, I described how capitalism inculcates ambition because people, upon its advent, could suddenly ascend the socio-economic hierarchy in ways they hadn't previously been able to. A son of working-class parents could theoretically save a lot of money from his wages and become a petit bourgeois small-business owner. It's in this desire to rise above the circumstances of one's birth that much capitalist ambition is cultivated. But the same possibility wasn't available to women until fairly recently. As I'll get to shortly, at the birth of capitalism men were forced into waged work in factories and farms, while most women were corralled into domestic work in the home, and if a woman did waged work, like manufacturing or cleaning, whatever money she made would usually go to her husband. If a woman's social standing improved, it was as a part of her family unit, whereas if a man's social standing improved, he could at least think it was a result of *his* individual ambition, hard work and thrift. Lady Macbeth remained the popular (and reviled) image of women's ambition for so long because she was able to manipulate her husband from the background, maintaining the illusion that he was the prime mover of their class mobility.

Women's ambition has become more acceptable since *Macbeth* was written. Much of the self-help material directed towards women encourages them to be ambitious in their professional lives. Though written for different audiences, books like *Lean In* and *#girlboss*, published in 2013 and 2014 respectively, accept the premise that women's lack of ambition is a product of social forces and seek to correct it by encouraging women to reach for the same kinds of career success as men. *Lean In* was directed towards the white-collar business world, imploring women to overcome the social and economic causes of their lack of ambition and develop the "will to lead", as the book's subtitle says. To "lean in" is to invest in a full-time ambitious career and not be a homemaker or a part-time employee. It's also to lean towards another, and affirm yourself, rather than lean out and abandon a potential career at the first sign of adversity. *#girlboss* is something like a more internet-savvy version of *Lean In*, directed towards millennial women who might not want a business career, but who want a sense of autonomy and economic independence. Ambitions of influencer-hood and internet entrepreneurship are their answer, and it's no small wonder why women on

Instagram rushed to proclaim themselves "girlbosses". There are legitimate reasons why women adopted the ethos of books like *Lean In* and *#girlboss*; in a world of increasing equality of opportunity between the genders, women want to be recognised for their work and have some autonomy over the course of their lives. But the vision offered in these books of individual women climbing the social ladder and becoming bosses — girl- or otherwise — isn't fulfilling for the majority of women.

In a book-length critique of *Lean In*, Dawn Foster accuses it — and *#girlboss*, by extension — of promoting a kind of "trickledown feminism", which works the same way as trickledown economics.[4] The premise of trickledown feminism is that gains solely experienced by wealthy and ambitious (and usually white) women in the worlds of business and politics are in fact gains for *all* women, irrespective of what these women do when put into positions of power and influence. Margaret Thatcher called feminism "poison",[5] defended powerful men like Jimmy Savile who preyed on young girls,[6] and cut social services, which left many women vulnerable,[7] but that doesn't stop her being referred to as a "real feminist" by those who see the business-class glass ceiling as the primary obstacle women face.[8] Upon Thatcher's death in 2013, Barack Obama commented that Thatcher was "an example to our daughters that there is no glass ceiling that can't be shattered", summarising the whole philosophy behind the trickledown feminism of *Lean In*'s author, Sheryl Sandberg.[9] Women in positions of power like Thatcher — or Hillary Clinton or Golda Meir or Taylor Swift[10] — become feminist icons not necessarily because they improve the lives of women but because their being in power supposedly shows women with wealth and privilege what they can accomplish. Their feminism is symbolic, in that they themselves are the symbols of what individual women, acting for and by themselves in an unequal economy, can achieve.

Nothing makes the internal contradictions of ambitious girlboss feminism clearer than a scandal Beyoncé was involved in in 2016, when it was revealed that her clothing brand, Ivy Park, used Sri Lankan sweatshop labour to make its clothes. A cover story about Ivy Park published in *Elle* positions the brand against other flash-in-the-pan celebrity businesses, and as a venture seeking to empower women: "[Ivy Park is] a way to push a feel-good, woman-power ethos, to de-emphasize perfectionism, to value strength over beauty, and to inspire, according to the company, 'women to work with, not against, their bodies'".[11] It turned out the strength of female empowerment only applied to the women buying the clothes, not the women in Sri Lanka being paid less than $1 an hour to make them while being barred from unionising.[12] If one were to make excuses for Ivy Park, one could say that the problem is with the entire fashion industry, and that it's awfully convenient to focus on a particular woman of colour rather than the fashion industry as a whole.[13] It is true that exploitation is an ongoing problem in the fashion industry, controversies around sweatshops have been a public issue at least since the 1990s, but what the Ivy Park saga shows is that contemporary liberal feminism has no interest in changing the nature of power or of ending exploitation; it only wants women holding the reins, rather than men. These *Lean In* and girlboss feminists cannot but be baffled by the question He Zhen, a Chinese anarchafeminist, asked more than a century ago: "If the majority of women do not want to be controlled by men, why would they want to be controlled by women?"[14]

Ironically, *Lean Out* and Beyoncé's sweatshop scandal highlight a kind of negative similarity between this book and the ambitious strains of feminism. By arguing against ambition, I suppose I'm trying to "close the ambition gap" just as much as Sandberg, but from the other direction. Rather than arguing for women to be more ambitious and to "lean in" to hegemonic masculinity and its ideal of individual career success, I'm arguing that everybody should be *less* ambitious and instead prioritise the reproductive labour which has traditionally been the domain of women.

Reproductive labour and its discontents

When I say "reproductive labour", usually the first thing that comes to mind for most people is childbirth. But while childbirth is an important part of reproductive labour, the term refers to much more than that. The broadest definition of the term refers to the labour which contributes to the reproduction of social, economic and natural conditions as distinguished from the labour contributing to the production of goods.[15] Cooking food, disposing of waste, raising children, planting trees: all these things fall under the remit of reproductive labour because they "reproduce humanity by taking care of the biophysical environment that makes life possible", as the ecofeminist Stefania Barca puts it.[16] If nobody disposed of waste, or raised children, there would be dire consequences, socially and economically. There wouldn't be a workforce without children, for starters, and waste gradually building up would lead to disease, infestation and negative environmental impacts on the area of the build-up. Reproductive labour is necessary to keep the human and non-human world alive, and yet it's completely devalued, socially and economically. But that hasn't always been the case.

Marxist feminists have long argued that reproductive work, and thus women's social and economic position, is uniquely devalued in capitalist society compared to previous economic arrangements. In feudal farms, for example, where work "was organized on a subsistence basis, the sexual division of labor […] was less pronounced and less discriminating than in a capitalist farm. In the feudal village *no social separation existed between the production of goods and the reproduction of the work-force*; all work contributed to the family's sustenance."[17] Men and women alike worked on farms for the sake of getting food on the table for their communities. And where there *was* a sexual division of labour between productive and reproductive labour, where women gave birth and men made bricks, neither gender was paid as compensation and the purpose of both was to ensure the survival of themselves and their community. But when feudal serfs were driven from their communal farms, with the men forced into factories and women into their homes, one gender's labour came to be compensated while the other's wasn't. "In the new monetary regime", Silvia Federici writes, "only production-for-market was defined as a value-creating activity, whereas the reproduction of the worker began to be considered as valueless from an economic viewpoint and even ceased to be considered as work."[18] And since the reproductive labour done by women was for the most part unpaid, they became economically dependent upon men in ways they previously hadn't been.

The social devaluing of reproductive labour is coupled with its economic devaluation. In other words, reproductive work almost always goes unpaid. Homemakers might work twenty hours one week and seventy hours the next, from 5am some days to 9pm on others. And the work is often unpleasant; there's not a lot of autonomy in cleaning a toilet, washing dishes or folding clothes. But there are no time-sheets to check how long they've worked, what they've done, and no payment for any of the time they've spent working. The rare occasion domestic labour is raised to the status of real work is when it's done in someone else's house for money. The work being done in these cases is mostly the same as that done by a homemaker in their own house, but since it's done for another family rather than one's own, and for money, it stops being a "natural" consequence of women's biology and begins to be work.

That money makes the difference between what is considered "real" and "fake" work isn't a coincidence. It's part of a deeper split in capitalism between use value (the utility of things and their ability to satisfy our needs) and exchange value (something's market price). Until fairly recently, use value was the only reason things were made or crops were grown. But with the advent of capitalism, all that changed, and things began to be made to be sold at the market for their exchange value. Suddenly, Marx writes in the *Grundrisse*, "production appears as the aim of mankind and wealth as the aim of production".[19] In other words, people exist to make things, and things are made not to be used but to be sold. With this shift came the economic and social devaluation of reproductive labour, which, in working to satisfy our wants and needs, (re)produces use value but produces no exchange value.[20] Dirty or torn clothes can't be worn, and cleaning clothes or sewing them back together recreates the use value lost when they were dirtied or torn. Moreover, cooking a good meal makes use value out of what used to be disparate, raw and inedible ingredients. But none of this work creates any *new* commodities to be bought and sold at the market, so it doesn't make any exchange value, and is thus invisible to our normal economic calculations.

The example of cooking helps tease out the differences between production and reproduction, exchange value and use value, and which of them is granted social and economic value. In an appearance on Conan O'Brien's talk show in 2009, Gordon Ramsay was teaching O'Brien and the comedian Norm Macdonald how to cook a dish that both comedians were struggling with. When Macdonald jokingly asked "Why would you become a cook?" Ramsay insisted, to some groans from the audience, that he was a *chef*, and that "ladies cook".[21] While more women are entering the world of professional cooking, in the UK in 2018, only 17 percent of chefs were women, giving the impression that traditional gender roles still determine who cooks what, for whom, and for what reason.[22]

For women of all sorts — homemakers, matriarchs, broke uni students — cooking is an act, perhaps *the* act, of reproductive labour. Very few things are more crucial to reproducing one's own and one's community's living conditions than cooked food. Whatever food is being cooked, from microwaveable noodles to rice and lentils to lamb roast, all of it is being cooked to satisfy the needs of oneself and one's milieu. Obviously, none of it is being sold. When I visit my family in my hometown, I usually end up cooking a large meal. I can't refuse my mother giving me money for groceries when I do, but even in cases like these where I'm given money to cook dinner, the money is for the ingredients, not the act of cooking dinner itself. It's much closer to reciprocating gifts than payment for a service.[23] If I wasn't given money for groceries, or if I managed to refuse vociferously enough, I wouldn't dare suggest my family pay me for the ingredients I bought or for my labour — that would be absurd. In keeping with the act of cooking as a gift to those eating, if there are leftovers, they're given free of charge.

For men who cook professionally, on the other hand, cooking food is an act of productive labour. The chef cooks a meal not to feed himself or other people but for the money that comes with selling that food for its exchange value on the market. Marx writes that as holders of exchange value, commodities "do not contain an atom of use-value".[24] What this means is that someone will only be willing to sell something if it has no utility, no use value, to them. A meal at a restaurant has use value to the person eating it then, but for the person making it, the chef, it's a commodity with an exchange value like any other, otherwise they'd sooner eat it themselves than sell it. I've been told restaurant staff eat a lot of leftovers, so perhaps when some food comes back later in the evening it might have some use value. But that doesn't change its nature as a commodity.

There's a further element of careerism and ambition to cheffing that isn't present when cooking food for oneself or one's loved ones. Chefs, who make commodities to be sold for their exchange value, can have lucrative careers — climbing up the ladder of their local restaurant scene from a dishwasher to a head chef at a well-reviewed restaurant, commanding a legion of sous chefs and line cooks and personally designing a menu, possibly even owning a restaurant themselves. If they have particularly high aspirations and a dramatic side, they could aim to be a celebrity chef like Gordon Ramsay, Anthony Bourdain or, in our era of nitrile glove-clad YouTube chefs, like Binging with Babish. Chefs can be ambitious because this avenue is potentially open for them if they should choose to pursue it. The same isn't true of homemakers and home cooks, who make food not to be sold for money but to be eaten for free. Not to brag, but I've made meals that people have said could be served at restaurants. Even so, there's no promotion waiting for me. There's no higher echelon of home cooks I can ascend to. All there is is another meal to make the next day.

There are good reasons why women are unhappy doing

reproductive labour. There's no money or recognition in it, and it must be a humiliating experience if you spend hours of every day catering for someone else's needs while they get the sole recognition for their successes. Women's career ambitions are, in part, a response to their dissatisfaction with existing in the background of men's lives and seemingly not having lives of their own. If a woman's labour is secondary to a man's, and supposedly exists to support *his* more important work, is it any wonder that women come out as less ambitious than men? If a woman wants to be economically independent, to be seen as a primary agent in her own life, she'll have to resist hundreds of years of history and socialisation, and to have career goals in addition to the reproductive labour she is already expected to do.

So why would I criticise women for being ambitious? Should women be content to remain supportive figures behind the men in their lives? This is, after all, why so many women rushed towards the *Lean In* and girlboss feminisms — because they were no longer happy being nothing more than a man's infrastructure, supporting him in the background, reproducing the conditions for his life while he chased his ambitions and his own success (of which he was recognised as the sole cause). But as this book has shown time and time again, ambition is a gilded cage, and is unable to provide the kind of liberation that women seek. The next section will draw on ecofeminist thought to show the solution isn't to offer women the "freedom" of careers, nor the "opportunity" to chase their ambitions and self-actualise through them In fact, it isn't women that need to change at all.

The work of nature: ecofeminism against ambition

The devaluing of women's reproductive work is taken even further when the reproductive labour done by women, undertaken for no pay, is regarded as a natural vocation instead of "real work". Because *some* kinds of reproductive labour are associated with biology — most of those born with vaginas are uniquely capable of "natural" childbirth and breastfeeding — "the rest of domestic work does not appear as work or labour".[25] Vacuuming, cooking, washing clothes and watering plants have nothing to do with biology — I'm a man and I do all these things more than my wife — yet they're lumped together with childbirth as the natural vocation of all women. A society influenced by feminism might recognise these things as being time-consuming and often quite strenuous, and it'd be correct to do so, but they're not regarded as work in the same way as productive labour for the sake of exchange value. Instead, reproductive labour is a "natural attribute of [women's] physique and personality, an internal need, an aspiration".[26]

While associations between vacuuming and women's "natural biology" are ridiculous, something shared between reproductive labour and natural processes is that neither creates commodities. Things only become commodities when they're "mixed" with human labour, since to become a commodity, "the product must be transferred to the other person, for whom it serves as a use value, through the medium of exchange".[27] The lemons hanging from my neighbour's tree don't have any exchange value, nor do they have any if I pluck a lemon and use it to make hummus. Something only has exchange value once it's been taken from this "state of nature" with the aim of exchanging it for something else. The same can be said for all those ancient forests in Europe being cut down and made into cheap IKEA furniture.[28] Until they're enclosed to be sold off to IKEA, those ancient forests have no exchange value. The "work" of growing all those trees has no economic value until people turn up with chainsaws and trucks to cut it all down. This is how, as Ariel Salleh writes it, the reproductive work of women came to be treated "like the rest of physical nature: air, streams, minerals and forests being tantamount to free goods".[29] In societies which prioritise exchange value, reproductive labour and natural processes exist to "build a taken-for-granted daily infrastructure" to be appropriated by productive labour.[30]

Contrary to contemporary feminists inspired by *Lean In* and its promises of high-profile careers for women, ecofeminists don't inherently see women's association with natural processes as a bad thing; we're all part of nature after all. What's bad is that women and the reproductive work they're socially assigned to do is devalued next to the work of men, which is regarded as something "above" nature. This isn't a problem with women, but with the economic system devaluing their work and the social consequences thereof. Men's work in the gendered division of labour isn't valued more highly than women's because it's more important, useful or necessary but because the kind of labour men are socialised to desire is the kind of labour capitalism recognises as economically valuable: productive labour in service of maximising exchange value. The "work" of nature and the kind of labour women are socialised to desire — reproductive labour in service of (re)producing use values — is no less necessary. In fact it's necessary if any productive labour is going to be done at all. IKEA furniture can't be made without the wood of those ancient forests. And those ancient forests can't be cut down without workers, who can only work if their clothes are clean, they eat a decent diet and were raised to have the social skills for working in a group setting.[31] The "eco" of ecofeminism stresses that women aren't naturally drawn to reproductive work any more than men, but that men have been socialised to abandon reproduction and the flows and fluxes of natural processes.

Ecofeminists are also correct in considering the ecological ramifications of productive labour for exchange value, the labour men are socialised to desire. It's productive (not reproductive) labour which contributes to the growing separation between the cyclic and regenerative metabolism of nature and the accumulative, growth-oriented labour of humans.[32] One example that's drawn particular attention is the industrialisation of agriculture and its effects on soil quality. For pre-capitalist economies, the purpose of agriculture was to grow enough food to meet people's nutritional needs, and the limited scale of agriculture, along with the "highly irrational and slothfully traditional way of working", allowed the soil to regenerate and remain nutrient-dense in the long term.[33] Humans worked with, and in, the natural processes of the soil, which met their needs while limiting their ecological impact. When the development of capitalism shifted the focus from meeting human needs to maximising profit, the scale of agriculture grew exponentially. In the short term this enabled large profits to be made by the early capitalist farms, who detected profit the way sharks detect blood in water, but it also led to the deterioration of the soil. When the capitalist farms recognised the deficient quality of their soil, they were so desperate to import fertiliser in the form of guano from South America that it led to the outbreak of war.[34] The ecological devastation wrought by capitalist production and the valorisation of exchange value over use value isn't a relic of the past.

The fast fashion trend demonstrates the environmental impact of our current economic system and how, in it, clothes are not made to be worn but to make money. Fast fashion involves popular brands identifying the latest fashion trends and making, distributing and selling the new clothes as quicky and as cheaply as possible. Since the point of fast fashion is to constantly change styles in keeping with whatever's popular, the clothes are not made to last, and most of them are destined for landfill in less than ten wears.[35] (A lot of clothes don't make it that far. A statistic from the Australian Circular Textiles Association states that about 30 percent of clothes made in the world are never worn.[36]) All this production has detrimental impacts on the environment, using large quantities of water and energy, dyeing water which runs off into streams and river, and using synthetic textiles like polyester which contribute to the spread of microplastics and require crude oil to be produced.[37] All this is a product of clothes not being made to be worn but to make money for the people who own stakes in large fast fashion brands like Forever 21 and Zara. As in the industrial agriculture example, every item of clothing being made requires working with and in the environment, since the fabric needs to come from *somewhere*. So long as clothes were made every so often when people actually needed them, the environmental cost remained low enough to be sustainable. But when production exists for the sake of exchange value and capital accumulation, this just isn't possible.

Furthermore, the economy works in such a way that companies often have no choice but to overproduce if they want to survive. If the early capitalist farmers didn't expand their operations to the detriment of the ecosystem, they would've quickly been outcompeted by farmers who *were* so willing. And if brands like H&M or Uniqlo refuse the trends of fast fashion, they'll lose the goodwill of profits and investors, which no company is willing to do.

Nothing demonstrates the compulsion of overproduction

better than the debacle surrounding the recent economic demise of the Instant Pot slow cooker. At the start of COVID-19, sales of the slow cookers spiked dramatically as more people were spending time in their homes. But a problem quickly arose: companies need a steady stream of profits, so how do you continue to sell slow cookers to people who already have one? Some companies might go the route of "planned obsolescence" and build their tech to break after a couple years of use. Others might offer subscription services, like many car manufacturers have taken to recently. One of the benefits of the Instant Pot is that it didn't attempt any of these transparent money-making strategies. Instead, as a headline in the *Atlantic* put it at the time, "The Instant Pot Failed Because It Was a Good Product".[38] For the company's short lifespan, the use value of its product outweighed its exchange value. By centring the reproduction of people's life-conditions rather than selling 2 to 4 percent more slow cookers every year, the Instant Pot met people's needs *too well*, and the company failed. Making durable products might not make economic sense, but it's obviously less detrimental to the environment than making products which need to be replaced every two years.

These environmental crises of overproduction are by no means caused by men's socialisation, but men's socialisation towards mastery and a refusal to recognise limits impacts how environmental problems are "solved". Men's socialisation shares an affinity with capitalism and ambition, seeing an environment as a situation to control and shape, not as something to live with/in.[39] The attitude is summed up by the first words in Martin Scorsese's *The Departed*, spoken by the mob boss played by Jack Nicholson: "I don't want to be a product of my environment. I want my environment to be a product of me." As such, the "solutions" supposedly remedying the environmental consequences of overproduction continue to misrecognise limits as obstacles, involve even more mastery over the natural world and do little but kick the can of ecological destruction down the road, onto future generations or to the Global South.

One of the most famous projects of environmental mastery from the nineteenth century was the mission to reverse the flow of the Chicago River to drive away the rapidly growing city's waste. The downside, however, was increased flooding in the river's new downstream zone — which had been productive farmland just months beforehand — and the environmental devastation caused by moving an entire city's sewage into waterways that served as animal habitats.[40] The reversal of the Chicago River is echoed today by cloud-seeding, the process of stimulating rainfall by dispersing sodium chloride, silver iodide or other chemicals into the atmosphere.[41] We don't yet know the long-term consequences of the cloud-seeding experiments done in the United Arab Emirates and other countries with low rainfall, but at the very least there are significant risks of air pollution from the chemicals and ecosystem destruction due to sudden increases of rainfall. For those who seek to master the environment and overcome its natural limits, any negative consequences to be experienced in the long term are less important than mitigating short-term impacts, and accomplishing the superhuman goal of making the environment bend to one's will.

Even within the left, there's a certain set of Promethean socialists — often ambitious technocrats in their own right — who get a little squeamish when they hear talk of ecological limits.[42] Much like ambitious capitalists, to them any recognition of limits sounds a little too much like defeatism and austerity.[43] But it's not defeatism to recognise the necessity and reality of ecological limits, the same way it isn't defeatism to say that, under natural conditions, water melts at 0 degrees and boils at 100 degrees. The historical malleability of what appears "natural" in human laws doesn't make actual natural laws malleable. As a recent book on degrowth puts it:

> The fact that ice melts beyond 0 degrees or that shells need calcium carbonate ($CaCO_3$) but that the absorption of CO_2 decreases carbonate ion (CO_3^{2-}) and increases bicarbonate ion (HCO_3^-) in the ocean is not something humans can determine nor modify according to their will, no matter how hard they try.[44]

Humans act on, in and with the non-human world, but that doesn't change the existence of hard and fast natural laws. There is no technocratic ambition that can overcome these limits.

We see in these examples how economic factors, coupled with the masculine attitude towards the environment — as an object of mastery, productivism and appropriation — lead to overproduction and ecological devastation, and how attempts at mitigating environmental damage cause their own problems. What Ariel Salleh calls women's "reproductive consciousness", the result of centuries of socialisation,[45] is clearly not the cause of these environmental problems, so it makes perfect sense that she and other ecofeminists would be wary of women abandoning their reproductive socialisation and aiming for the same careers as men if these are the consequences. Do we really need more ambitious people looking to exert their economic will on the world without consideration of the ecological damage? With these crises of overproduction in mind, do we need more entrepreneurs starting clothing brands of their own? Do we need repeats of the Chicago River reversal looking to create "a good, or even great, Anthropocene", as the authors of *An Ecomodernist Manifesto* put it?[46] The problem lies in the fact that everybody is invariably "in/with/of nature", but it's men who have been socialised to be ambitious, to separate themselves from the environment and its cyclical processes of regeneration and reproduction, and to instead treat the environment as either a free resource to appropriate or an obstacle to master.[47]

This is why, to my mind, materialist ecofeminism is the best response to the hierarchised binaries described so far in this chapter. Ecofeminists accept women's socialisation as more reproductive than productive, less ambitious, more mindful of externalities, and as involving a work process more in line with that of the non-human environment.[48] Unlike the *Lean In* feminists described early in this chapter, they don't see women's socialisation as the problem. The problems are the gendered division of labour demarcating men's and women's work as "naturally" distinct, and that the reproductive work women are socially assigned to do in this division of labour is devalued compared to the work of men. The ecofeminist solution to women's dissatisfaction with reproductive labour isn't to stoke their ambitions and get them into high-paying profit-driven careers, but to eliminate the gendered division of labour and prioritise reproductive labour and use values.

Since some things will still need to be made, some productive labour will always have to occur, but production will be subject to what Kohei Saito describes as "degrowth communism".[49] What this means is that instead of the situation today, where reproduction is subordinated to production, in degrowth communism productive labour would be subordinate to reproduction.[50] In other words, instead of reproducing people and nature because they can be directed towards profit-making, the task of production would be to sustainably reproduce the conditions of people and their non-human environment. Hammers, clothes and machines would be made because people need them to live, not because selling them is a profitable enterprise. Or, as Marx put it in the *Grundrisse*, whereas in capitalist societies "production appears as the aim of mankind and wealth as the aim of production", in these economies "it is the actual community and its conditions that presents itself as the basis of production, *the reproduction of this community being production's final purpose*".[51]

With these ecofeminist priorities, women's socialised lack of ambition would no longer be perceived as a deficiency but as a social good. If someone wanted to pursue their career ambitions, the social response wouldn't be to heap praise upon them, but to question them and their motives — for as we've seen throughout this chapter, ambition occurs at the expense of social reproduction. If the point of an economy was to create use values and reproduce the conditions for the flourishing of the human and non-human environment, what would be the point of starting fashion brands or start-ups or dropshipping operations? We have more than enough of these things today, and they don't reproduce people's ability to live. They're much more concerned with making money, and a lot of them barely manage that. The unambitious everyday acts of reproductive labour — cooking meals, cleaning toilets, sweeping streets, caring for children and the elderly — are what reproduce us and our conditions, and they are the acts to be socially valorised.

7. Wasting Our Potential

The Idler, who habituates himself to be satisfied with what he can most easily obtain, not only escapes labours which are often fruitless, but sometimes succeeds better than those who despise all that is within their reach, and think every thing more valuable as it is harder to be acquired.
                              — Samuel Johnson, "The Idler's Character"[1]

Birds flying high, you know how I feel,
Sun in the sky, you know how I feel,
Breeze driftin' on by, you know how I feel.
                              — Nina Simone, "Feeling Good"

An ambitious life is one of purpose and economic maximisation, and involves realising a direction in our lives while getting as much money as we can. A non-ambitious life would then characterised by aimlessness and waste. Lives such as these are looked down upon today, cast not only as morally corrupt but also as economically irresponsible. "Shouldn't you be trying to find your purpose or working on your career?" they might ask, a little suspiciously, "You'd make more money if you put more effort in and worked a little harder." But as the previous chapter shows, some of the most crucial work that exists today is paid badly, with little to no built-in career prospects or sense of direction inherent to it, less concerned with creating new commodities than it is with reproducing the living conditions of people and their environment. If a non-ambitious society was to make social reproduction the primary form of labour, its aimless and non-productive qualities would be understood as a benefit, not a defect. This chapter will gesture towards a non-ambitious life by putting a positive spin on these qualities.

Positively Rudderless

There are all sorts of words used to morally tar a person or an institution with no sense of direction or purpose: "directionless", "adrift", "aimless". "Rudderless" is a personal favourite of mine because its etymological roots cut to the heart of what purpose and direction are all about.

The word "rudderless" comes from sailing terminology, the rudder being the instrument one steers to turn the boat in the water. A rudderless boat is a boat not just without a sense of direction, but without an instrument which could provide it with a sense of direction. This is why, if we want to discuss what a non-ambitious life might look like, I find "rudderless" to be a more useful word than "aimless" or "purposeless" or, if I'm feeling fancy, "ateleological". A boat might not have a direction, but it might still have a rudder, something that can be taken and used to give a direction should someone see fit to do so. A boat without a rudder, like life after capitalism, doesn't even have the *capacity* to be given direction. Direction has been "deprived of its foundation", to reuse a phrase from a couple chapters back. Without a rudder, the boat drifts freely.

And who is it that steers the rudder exactly? I'm hardly the first person to point out that the words "steersman" and "government" have the same etymological root, going all the way back to ancient Greece. That hardly seems like a coincidence when we compare the two side by side. Just as the government can be understood as an instrument or institution to *steer* people towards law and order and what are supposedly their best interests, the steersmen on a boat are the ones *governing* the boat's direction across the water. If to be governed is to be given a direction, even by ourselves, living rudderless lives might be one more way we can live by that old anarchist mantra of "becoming ungovernable".

But living a rudderless life comes with economic risk. The precarity of work encourages us to specialise in something — *anything* — as early as we can so that we'll be in the most advantageous position to compete against everybody else vying for a slice of the economic pie. Someone who likes to read or to cook or to do handyman activities will be in the best position for the job market if they get exceptionally good at reading texts, cooking or DIY work as early as they can. I like doing all these things, and despite the economic benefits, I don't want to become an academic, a chef or a professional handyman. Those of us who don't want to find careers, who don't want to invest in ourselves and our earning potential and who want to engage in activities without turning them into profitable enterprises, are left economically precarious. As the popular metaphor says, if you're stationary while the world moves forwards, you're moving backwards.

Perhaps because of its economic non-utility, rudderlessness also comes with moral condemnation. Either there's something wrong with the rudderless and they should be pathologised, or they just haven't yet found their true calling. If one googles phrases regarding the topic of purposelessness, aimlessness or lack of higher meaning in their life, the top results will often be for depression and psychological services (at least this is true in Australia). If not, it'll be Reddit posts or self-help blogs all about the value of finding purpose and bestowing one's life with a sense of meaning. When I was in my late teens and early twenties, working night shifts at my local supermarket and hanging out with my friends when I had the chance, I would sometimes be told by people, "You should put your intelligence to good use." These people were obviously well-meaning — they were complimenting me, after all — but their tone often came with an implicit criticism, not just of me, but also of the people I worked with, who were intelligent people in their own right. The implication is always that if someone is living a rudderless life and doesn't intend to give themselves a sense of direction or purpose, either economic conditions or psychological counselling will step in and force their hand.

There may be a great deal of work being put in to make people find their sense of purpose and direction, but as the previous chapter showed, most work which holds the world together — the work of social reproduction, not of value production — is done by people whose work has no sense of direction, or possibility of career advancement or even particularly good pay.

A recent film — Wim Wenders's *Perfect Days* — showcases the directionless work necessary for social reproduction. The film's protagonist, Hirayama, who works as a toilet cleaner in Tokyo, does the exact same work nearly every day with no expectation nor desire for career advancement. Where a lesser film might use toilet cleaning as the "rags" portion in a linear rags-to-riches narrative, *Perfect Days* is content to show the aimless repetition of Hirayama's existence. As such, the film has very little in the way of plot or narrative and is instead a series of brief episodes or encounters which occur during the course of Hirayama's working week. In one episode, his niece runs away from home and lives with him for a couple days. In another, Hirayama plays noughts and crosses (or tic-tac-toe) with an unseen person who leaves a piece of paper in a stall. Nothing happens as a result of either of these episodes other than the experiences themselves; Hirayama's niece is eventually returned to her mother and the noughts and crosses game is a draw. There's nothing especially exciting to recall about the film, but its strengths are in the experience of watching it, true to the movie's goal of highlighting the profundity of the everyday. Though in the world of film, *Perfect Days* is an exception.

Film is for the most part highly directional; besides *Perfect Days*, it has little of the rudderless about it. It's about characters, what they want and their interactions with each other on the way to getting what they want. The defining characteristic of film, particularly genre films, is the "MacGuffin": the meaningless plot device instantly providing a motivation for every character in a story, seen in everything from *Dune* to *The Avengers* to *Raiders of the Lost Ark*. Film is set on following that piece of writing advice from Kurt Vonnegut, who said, "Every character should want something, even if it is only a glass of water."[2] Considering any popular film quickly makes this point obvious. *Dune*'s Paul Atreides wants to avenge the death of his father and sabotage his chief enemy's resource extraction, taking it for himself. *Halloween*'s Laurie Strode wants to escape the murderous clutches of Michael Myers. Both works waste no time in divulging what their characters want. Much like the characters themselves, everything has a purpose, and there's little that isn't relevant to the plot.

The same is not true of literature. Tom Lutz is correct in writing that while "the genre novel is on a mission [...]. Literature on a whole is aimless."[3] I think aimlessness is better captured in novel form than on film, where description can take precedence over individual characters and their narrativisation. *Pride and Prejudice*, for example, consists mostly of people going to balls and gossiping about their marriage prospects. Much to my dismay when I first read it as a teenager, the plot is little more than "a woman and a man make a bad first impression and grow to love each other". Even more-recent literary works showcase the often aimless experience of everyday life. *My Year of Rest and Relaxation* is a novel of recent note, almost entirely set in a New York City apartment while its well-off protagonist slowly withers away on a variety of sleeping pills. The plot is threadbare, and the fact that it features the 9/11 attacks as its climactic moment serves to remind readers just how directionless the whole book is. Where genre fiction has its MacGuffins and complex plot summaries, the defining characteristic of literature is its divergences and its deviances, its asides and its anecdotes.[4]

The novel which best expresses literature's aimlessness is, to my mind, *Moby-Dick*. While the novel is named after its supposed "goal" (the eponymous white whale), *Moby-Dick* is (in)famous for its aimless, wandering quality. It's over six hundred pages long, and I think less than a quarter of those are dedicated to the hunt for Moby Dick — maybe less than a tenth, in fact. It seems the narrator, Ishmael, would much prefer to remark upon anything else: the different uses for whale products; how unreliable sailors are; all the different kinds of whales, and how all the species might be put into a schema. On and on it goes. The novel's namesake only turns up for the final three chapters of the book, a total of about thirty pages in my edition.

And much like his narration, Ishmael himself doesn't appear to have any real sense of purpose in the novel. When asked by one of the *Pequod's* owners why he wants to go whaling, Ishmael can only answer with a non-committal shrug: "Well, sir, I want to see what whaling is. I want to see the world."[5] And this is no chance comment from Ishmael. He quickly separates himself from other sailors of his experience by telling the reader he has no desire to ascend the ranks and turn whaling into a career:

> No, I never go as a passenger; nor, though I am something of a salt, do I ever go to sea as a Commodore, or a Captain, or a Cook. I abandon the glory and distinction of such offices to those who like them. For my part, I abominate all honorable respectable toils, trials, and tribulations of every kind whatsoever.[6]

Ishmael's sailing isn't due to a grand sense of purpose, or an existential quest to discover himself. He's doing it because he likes it, he's good at it, and because he simply wants to. He needs no additional motivation. Not only is Ishmael purposeless in his own motives, but he warns the reader against those "formed for noble tragedies", Shakespearean heroes whose ambition is their own undoing, who forget or ignore that "all mortal greatness is but disease".[7]

Ishmael's captain, the monomaniacal Ahab, is *Moby-Dick*'s counterpoint to Ishmael's rudderlessness, the novel's Shakespearean hero. Ahab's quest to avenge his missing leg by killing the whale that took it exemplifies the madness of a life dedicated to one's purpose: "The path to my fixed purpose is laid with iron rails", Ahab says to himself, "whereon my soul is grooved to run."[8] Ahab spends most of his time alone in his cabin, obsessively poring over charts and maps of the oceans and each of their currents. He doesn't sleep, nor does he socialise with his crew. In case it wasn't obvious enough,

Ahab himself makes it clear that not only is he unhappy, but his clarity of purpose makes him incapable of happiness:

> Oh! time was, when as the sunrise nobly spurred me, so the sunset soothed. No more. This lovely light, it lights not me; all loveliness is anguish to me, since I can ne'er enjoy [...]; damned, most subtly and most malignantly! damned in the midst of Paradise![9]

Like Prometheus, to whom the narrator compares Ahab in a later chapter, Ahab's purpose has turned him into a pitiful creature, doomed to eternal suffering.[10] Rather than a source of happiness and freedom, as a life of purpose is depicted today, Ahab's purpose is instead a millstone around his neck.

It shouldn't be forgotten that Ahab is the boss of his ship, and thus can only accomplish his purpose with the help of his crew. A large part of his job, then, is the same as that of any other boss: to ensure his crew works effectively by internalising his purpose and assuming it as their own.[11] And it's not an easy task, for as the book says, sailors "are more or less capricious and unreliable", aimless drifters like Ishmael, who won't hesitate to abandon ship for greener pastures should opportunity strike.[12]

Ahab is mostly successful, too. The only person who doesn't submit to Ahab's purpose in hunting Moby Dick is his first mate, Starbuck. When Ahab first lays out the nature of his mission — his purpose not to make a profit but to hunt one particularly dangerous whale — Starbuck is the only one to respond with any sort of hesitation, saying, "I came here to hunt whales, not my commander's vengeance."[13] The only reason Starbuck doesn't totally adopt Ahab's purpose is because he has a purpose of his own: to make money and return safely to his wife and son. This nascent conflict bubbles under the surface of much of the novel, but it only comes to a direct confrontation later on, when costly whale oil leaks and safe repairs require stopping the hunt for Ahab's whale. Starbuck argues that continuing Ahab's quest risks losing

> "in one day more oil than we may make good in a year. What we come twenty thousand miles to get is worth saving, sir."
> "So it is, so it is; if we get it."
> "I was speaking of the oil in the hold, sir."
> "And I was not speaking or thinking of that at all."[14]

But by this point Ahab is a successful boss; he has the full support of his crew, and the lone insubordination of Starbuck is easily smothered. Ahab is certainly the kind of man "formed for noble tragedies" of which Ishmael writes, but the real tragedy is that by *Moby-Dick*'s conclusion the Pequod's crew all fall under Ahab's spell.

And at the end of the novel, what does Ahab's monomania accomplish? For all his raving about glory and revenge, to what end does he ultimately sacrifice not only his life, but those of his crew? After the final confrontation, Moby Dick escapes, the *Pequod* is destroyed beyond repair and Ishmael is the only crewmember alive. The final sentence of the novel (besides Ishmael's epilogue) demonstrates just how futile Ahab's mad quest ultimately is: "Then all collapsed, and the great shroud of the sea rolled on as it rolled five thousand years ago".[15] The sea rolls on as if nothing has changed, because nothing has. Even if he had killed Moby Dick and achieved his purpose, Ahab's life, defined by a single purpose, couldn't possibly have made any difference to the unthinkably vast expanse of the ocean. Like Ozymandias's statue found as "two vast and trunkless legs of stone" in the desert,[16] Ahab's glory would eventually crumble until it was as if he was never there.

The aimlessness of *Moby-Dick* garnered Melville a great deal of criticism when the novel was originally published. Even those critics celebrating Melville's excellent prose reacted negatively to the novel's divergences, which one critic called its "lawless flights".[17] Where more-popular literature of the day was able to fit into one stable category, *Moby-Dick* eschewed many genre conventions, becoming what another critic called "an intellectual chowder of romance, philosophy, natural history, fine writing, good feeling, bad sayings".[18] It seems as though these critics would have much preferred a book narrated by Ahab than by Ishmael. They, like Ahab, have no time for anything which detracts from the quest to hunt the white whale. They either weren't able or weren't interested to grasp the fact that the novel isn't a failed adventure story but a study in aimlessness and an excoriation of subordinating oneself to a purpose.

One of the contemporaneous criticisms which remains true to this day is that the book is "extravagant" in its style.[19] And it's true, the book does much more than it strictly needs to in order to communicate its plot, which could be summarised in a paragraph or two. Characters' ravings to themselves and others take up many of the novel's six-hundred-plus pages, and Ishmael's personal feelings on a variety of topics don't need to be there. A novel doesn't strictly *need* to dedicate several pages to why a whale's tail is such an impressive thing to see with one's own eyes. With all its aimlessness and its excess, *Moby-Dick* could accurately be described as wasteful. But as the next section will explain, wastefulness, like aimlessness, can be quite a good thing indeed.

Waste and Sovereignty

What does it mean to "waste" something, or to be "wasteful"? A person with no interest in literature could say that reading a novel like *Moby-Dick* is a waste of time. It can be said that I waste my money buying the occasional bottle of wine, or second-hand books that I'll probably never get around to reading. Food waste, the discarding of perfectly edible food, has become a massive crisis, large enough to capture the attention of environmental NGOs, the UN, world governments and charitable organisations.

Waste is by necessity a comparative assessment. Saying something is "wasted" is an implicit suggestion that whatever that thing is, it could be used more productively. Think back to an earlier chapter of this book, when I mentioned my old anthropology professor who used to bake us banana bread with bananas he'd saved from a dumpster. He prevented those bananas from going to waste by using them to feed us instead. E-waste workers in Ghana expose themselves to all manner of toxic chemicals when they save all our electronic components from being wasted by rifling through the components we so thoughtlessly throw away.[20] We might refer to the lives of those Ghanian workers as "wasted" when we realise there's something else they might have preferred to be doing if they had been given the chance. There are good reasons as to why we tend to cast waste in a negative light.

But as I hinted at above, waste isn't universally a bad thing. Many of our everyday actions could be described as wasteful if looked at under a microscope. My money is wasted if I spend it on wine and books because, theoretically, I could use it to buy cheap proteins like lentils in bulk quantities and make myself meals for a month. Or I could invest it in a reliable index fund. That hypothetical person calling *Moby-Dick* a waste of time is kind of right, in that a person's time could be spent more productively than reading a fictional book that's more than a century old. I read most of *Moby-Dick* while I was on holiday in Queensland, wasting my time reading on the beach when I could have been at home working. Or if I *had* to spend my time reading on the beach, I could've been reading a business management self-help book instead. Airports sell plenty of them, too.

This is the kind of waste which drew the interest of the French philosopher Georges Bataille. Wasteful consumption, as opposed to productive consumption, is for Bataille central not just to our economy but to all economies throughout history.

Bataille understood that when we take as a starting point the sun and the functionally limitless supply of energy it produces, economic affairs are characterised by an immense *excess* of resources rather than by the scarcity often imagined by traditional economists. When we zoom out far enough and consider all life on earth as a totality rather than a multitude composed of individual plants and animals struggling for survival, we see that the sun produces far more energy than the minimal amount anything actually needs to survive. More food can be grown with the sun's energy than can ever be eaten. And since species can't help but consume this excess energy when presented with it, they either grow in individual size, increase their population, or find ways to expend that energy unproductively — to *waste it*. Bataille is chiefly concerned with the question of "how the wealth is to be squandered".[21]

What are some of the ways in which these excess resources

can be wasted? Art and monuments are some of the finest human examples of "those sudden openings beyond the world of useful works".[22] We all know someone who talks about art in purely economic terms, who never fails to mention how much money is *wasted* for the sake of art. The money could always be put to better use funding governmental services or foreign military exploits, and these complaints will often turn up in local newspapers. In the 1970s, there was a minor scandal in Australia when its centre-left government spent over one million dollars on Jackson Pollock's "Blue Poles". It was seen as a fiscally irresponsible move, indicative of a government willing to waste too much of its taxpayers' money. Waste is often put in monetary terms, but art doesn't need to be expensive to be wasteful. Punk bands who play free shows in shitty venues are wasting their time as well as their energy, transforming both into what Bataille called "the effervescence of life".[23] For punk bands, Jackson Pollock and the Australian government, there's always something more productive they could've been doing.

Regarding monuments, there's no better example than the pyramids. We look at them today as feats of engineering and archaeological curiosities (or grounds for conspiracy theory), but if we're to inhabit a purely utilitarian and economic understanding of the world, aren't they also a massive waste of resources? How much labour, human and animal, was required to build the pyramids? Could it not have been spent farming or fishing instead, which would've increased Ancient Egypt's population and perhaps contributed to its imperial expansion? Putting aside the question of labour, what about those masses of limestone and granite? The resources put towards constructing the pyramids could have built houses, bridges or fortresses instead. We know now that the pyramids served as tombs for Ancient Egypt's pharaohs and their worldly possessions, but the same function could be served by a bunker in the desert. I think we can all admit that seeing the world this way leads to some depressing conclusions.

This reminds me of a story my mother told me about my late grandfather when I was a kid. As the story goes, my grandfather was visiting Rome with his wife, my grandmother, and when they saw the Colosseum, my grandfather's immediate reaction was to ask something along the lines of "Why don't they knock it down and build real estate there instead?" Obviously, this is an absurd thing to suggest, but my grandfather's comment brings the utilitarian ethos into sharp relief when he considers a structure built nearly two thousand years ago to be a waste of land. Not content to be a waste of human and animal labour during their construction, monuments can also waste land in the present!

Animals can't make art or build colosseums, but they have their own ways of squandering excess energy. Meerkats spend a great deal of their time playing with each other, constantly wrestling in the sand rather than doing more economically productive activities like foraging for food or resting. Because wrestling is energy-intensive, scientists usually assume that there must be some functional justification for meerkats' playfulness. One theory, called the "social cohesion hypothesis", suggests that playing together strengthens the meerkats' social relationships. But when this was tested, it showed that there was no correlation between meerkats' playing and their social conditioning,[24] nor was there any reduction of aggression.[25] Another theory could be that physical playing teaches animals skills which could help them survive in the wild, but when that theory was tested on kittens, it, too, showed no correlation.[26] All this research has gone into uncovering what playing *doesn't do* for the animal kingdom, but we have at least some knowledge of what it *does do*. Like the Egyptians building pyramids or Jackson Pollock with his paintbrushes, playing consumes the excess energy of meerkats in a non-productive way.

People might have some problems with the examples I used above. After all, the Giza pyramids and the Colosseum in Rome were built using slave labour. The fact that one class (the slaves) was forced to produce wealth without consuming it, while the other (the rulers) consumed that wealth without producing it, is the fulcrum around which Bataille's definition of sovereignty bends. For Bataille, what distinguishes sovereignty from its opposite, servility, is that "the sovereign individual consumes and doesn't labor, whereas at the antipodes of sovereignty the slave and the man without means labor and reduce their consumption to the necessities, to the products without which they could neither subsist nor labor".[27] Or to put it more simply, the servile are left with the bare necessities they need to survive, while the sovereign are those living off the fruits of others' labour.

In feudal and slave economies, the servile–sovereign split ran along class lines fairly simply, but the development of capitalism and the internalisation of the new bourgeois ethos complicated matters. The non-working classes of feudalism — the lords, monarchs, church officials, etc. — didn't have to reinvest in what they owned, so they weren't economically compelled to accumulate capital to expand their business interests. They could maintain their incomes through collecting rent and taxes without the growth imperative which would come later in capitalist economies. This meant that if an economic surplus did emerge, it could be spent unproductively without putting anything at stake. Festivals, jubilees, art and monuments are the waste products of this feudal surplus. The bourgeoisie, on the other hand, *had* to accumulate capital if they were to reinvest, grow and survive long-term. It thus became imperative for the bourgeoisie to ensure their surplus was consumed productively, "to devote their resources to the installation of workshops, factories or mines".[28] This meant any surplus couldn't be put towards monuments or festivals, but was instead squirrelled away as a future reinvestment fund. Because the bourgeoisie are so tied to their drive to accumulate and the necessity of productivity, the distinction between who is sovereign and who is servile is very blurred indeed.

Rich people today are, after all, often praised for their supposed hard work and their frugality, which are for Bataille the characteristics of the servile. Before his reputation suffered a blow for the disastrous purchase of Twitter, Elon Musk was celebrated for spending nights sleeping on the floor of a Tesla factory instead of kicking back with his feet up on a private island.[29] Less out of necessity and more as a motivational tool for his employees, who would be convinced to work harder if they knew their boss was doing it too, Musk was nonetheless praised by business types for his supposed sacrifice and his willingness to spend a few days smelling like metal shavings. Warren Buffett is another example of a billionaire praised for slumming it, equally famous for his wealth and his thrift. The same business rags heaping praise upon Elon Musk are quick to celebrate Buffett for all the different ways he saves money, like living in the same house in Nebraska for half a century, eating McDonalds for breakfast and spending his time playing bridge rather than hunting endangered animals.[30]

Against self-help books, hustle-culture YouTube videos and finance magazines, the Bataillean understanding of sovereignty would regard these anecdotes about Musk and Buffett with absolute disdain. For what's the point of all that money if they're not going to actually enjoy any of it? As I've said already in this book, the point of money for capitalists isn't to enjoy it at all; they live as little more than conduits for the accumulation of capital. As much of their money as possible needs to be invested and reinvested, and any private consumption of theirs effectively reduces their own ability to reinvest.[31] This is the opposite of sovereignty, as Bataille conceives it, since the actions of the ultra-wealthy like Musk and Buffett are founded upon self-denying asceticism and completely tied to the motions of the economy. There has developed among capitalists, as Marx writes in the first volume of *Capital*, "a Faustian conflict between the passion for accumulation and the desire for enjoyment", and to this day it's considered responsible business practice to tamp down that desire for enjoyment as much as one possibly can.[32]

If rich people subordinate themselves to the economy, does that mean Bataille thinks that the proletariat are completely sovereign agents? No, obviously not, but we are more than capable of minor acts, small moments of unproductive expenditure, which reveal our potential for sovereignty. One such example, one that Bataille specifically draws upon, is someone drinking a glass of wine at the end of the day.[33] We might say we're drinking alcohol for all sorts of reasons — to relax, to socialise, to get through another day of work — but what we're ultimately doing, no matter what, is consuming something unproductively. We might joke otherwise, but we don't *need* to drink wine to live, so drinking wine is beyond the subsistence-level consumption Bataille says is representative of slaves. We're not drinking because it'll make us better at our jobs, like those tech workers taking small quantities of LSD to boost their productivity.[34] We're using our money to buy some wine we have no productive use for — wasting our money, really — and we're drinking for nothing more than our personal enjoyment.

While typical judgements of social activity imply "that all individual effort, in order to be valid, must be reducible to the fundamental necessities of production and conservation", Bataille's thinking is unique for turning this principle on its head.[35] The impetus of the economy is not production or conservation of energy but *non*production and the *wasting* of energy. But it's not only products which can be wasted and squandered. One of the chief commodities of capitalism is time, which can be wasted too.

Wasting Our Potential

As I've already said, wastefulness is often criticised as either an economic or moral defect of the wasteful person. We might ask ourselves why we'd bother spending money on a nice dinner at a good restaurant rather than cook something cheaper at home. And if we buy the nice dinner anyway, it might be accompanied by feelings of guilt. We might feel bad reminding ourselves how the money spent could've bought so many litres of fuel for our car. Nowhere is the sense of economic and moral guilt tied to waste more apparent than in the phenomenon of wasted time.

Even though he was writing more than a century before the "grindset" culture this book is largely responding to, Marx's writing about the length of the working day remains invaluable if we want to think seriously about the economics of wasting time. Writing about the development of shiftwork and manufacturing, Marx notes that a capitalist who rents a factory for a year is by nature renting the factory for the whole twenty-four hours of every day in that year. If they want to squeeze the most profit out of their investment, they need to keep that factory running for the full twenty-four hours. "In so far as the means of production fail to do this, their mere existence forms a loss for the capitalist, in a negative sense, for while they lie fallow they represent a useless advance of capital."[36] In other words, if a factory is only used for ten hours a day, the capitalist has, in essence, lost the remaining fourteen potential hours of every day that they've already paid for. I'll grant that, by itself, this isn't that interesting an observation. I've worked the dreaded night shift myself, and anyone familiar with factory labour will understand this intuitively. What gives Marx's statement its force is the insinuation that once the upkeep for something has been paid for a full day, if that thing is left dormant, even for a moment, it's time that has been wasted.

Human capital theory encourages us to see ourselves as a kind of factory, just one more form of capital to invest in and from which to extract the maximum profits available. The comparisons don't end there. The same way factories are paid for and maintained by the capitalist, the human body has biological demands if it's going to be reliable. We need food, water, shelter, other people and a host of other things that change from culture to culture if we're going to live. And like a factory, the human body is maintained for the full twenty-four hours a day, not counting the hours spent sleeping. Anyone interested in maximising the profits of their human capital must come to the troubling realisation that unless they're being economically useful every waking moment of every day, they are in effect *losing money* in the way Marx describes.

And because, as the sociologists Luc Boltanski and Ève Chiapello argue, "time is a resource that cannot be stored", the threat of wasted time is always lurking in the background of our daily activities.[37] You can save money by not spending it on nice dinners or rare collectible CDs, but you can't squirrel away time in a bank account. I do the majority of the housework in my house, and if I suddenly cut down the time spent doing those odd jobs from two hours to one, I haven't "saved" an hour, because I can't just put that extra hour away for a rainy day like one can do with money. What I've actually done is I've *freed* up an hour of my time which I can then spend watching crappy self-help videos on YouTube or investing in cryptocurrency instead of sweeping the floor, doing laundry and cleaning the toilet. Unlike money, time is always being consumed, without fail,[38] so to "save" time doesn't only mean to spend every hour productively, it also requires always aiming for the maximum productivity one can achieve, to always be doing more with less time.

As you can imagine, this leads to some truly bizarre attitudes towards time and productivity on the part of those driven by their ambition. Attempting to squeeze maximum productivity out of every moment makes time into a threat one has to conquer. The hustle-culture motivational speaker Ed Mylett tells us with his trademark enthusiasm that "the elite performers look at time and use time completely differently than the people who perform at an average level."[39] And he's right, for the example he provides boggles the mind:

> My day is 6am to noon. [...] My second day starts at noon and goes till 6pm. [...] And then the next day is 6pm to midnight. What I've done now is I have changed and manipulated time. I now get twenty-one days a week. Stack that up over a month, I'm gonna kick your butt. Stack it up over a year, you're toast. Stack it up over five years, my entire life is different than it would've been otherwise.[40]

This statement is ridiculous on its face. It might remind you, as it did me, of that old joke about someone who wants their pizza cut into six slices rather than eight because they're too full to eat eight slices of pizza. The pizza is the same size no matter how many slices it's cut into, and a day marks the amount of time the Earth spins on its axis, no matter how productive a person is during that period. A less strange way of articulating Mylett's statement is that he aims to be as productive in a six-hour period as other people are in an eighteen-hour period. The internet may have made fun of Mylett for his "twenty-one-day week" statement, but a large portion of the population have internalised his ethos nonetheless.

The ambitious are keenly aware of the twenty-four hours they have in each day. If they're to succeed in their life's goal, they need to use every moment effectively and with purpose. If they want to be an entrepreneur, they might spend long nights writing emails, soliciting investors or reading books written about those they'd like to emulate. If they want to own a small local business, they might be poring over spreadsheets, perfecting their craft or networking with others in their area. You might think people like this don't sleep much, but in a strange twist, sleep has been a recent area of interest in the culture of maximising productivity, as if sleep is only justifiable on the grounds that it makes us more productive.[41]

Ambition's orientation towards the future also comes into play as it relates to time. Even though Benjamin Franklin was wrong on the specificities when he wrote that "time is money", the two are similar in that when we look into the distant future, our current actions have an outsized impact on where we might end up.

Remember, that money is of the prolific, generating nature. Money can beget money, and its offspring can beget more, and so on. Five shillings turned is six, turned again it is seven and threepence, and so on, till it becomes a hundred pounds. The more there is of it, the more it produces every turning, so that the profits rise quicker and quicker. *He that kills a breeding sow, destroys all her offspring to the thousandth generation. He that murders a crown, destroys all that it might have produced, even scores of pounds.*[42]

This is also something Ed Mylett's "six-hour days" rant expresses as well. The economic benefits of maximised productivity become clearer when extrapolated over an entire lifespan, or even further, until Franklin's "thousandth generation". Suddenly, the week spent beachside reading *Moby-Dick* isn't only a week's worth of productivity wasted; one has also wasted all the potential returns (and reinvestments and rereturns) which that week's productivity could have generated, *ad infinitum*. Ambition's futurity constrains us not only through purpose and productivity, but also in our willingness to subordinate our present time to our potential futures.

This idea holds a certain personal resonance for me, since I went to university later than I was expected to and I've still avoided finding myself a "calling" or something I'm willing to call a career. But I'm not going to pretend that going to university earlier, or discovering my interest in writing sooner, wouldn't have been economically beneficial. I could've spent my early twenties trying to break into the competitive world of academia rather than working in a supermarket, and that certainly could've granted me more pay than what I get now.

But if the brief time I spent around career academics is any indication, I would've had less free time to engage in my hobbies and just enjoy my life.

There's a famous quote attributed to Bertrand Russell which claims that "the time you enjoy wasting is not wasted time." I fully agree with the sentiment that wasted time is often time we enjoy, but I disagree with Russell's insistence that this somehow stops that time from being a waste. As I've already indicated, I enjoyed wasting my early twenties on socialising, travelling and the occasional drug use, but I'm not going to pretend that time was spent productively, even by the twists of hustle-culture logic which turn everything one does into a productivity hack. During that time, I wasn't interested in being productive; I was working as little as I could get away with, and given that my job offered little in the way of a career, I was unconcerned about my future. I don't think it's *despite* these things that I was happy; I think it's *because* I wasn't concerned about the future, and *because* I wasn't being productive, that I was happy. And because of these things I'm still happy now.

This resonates with the underappreciated temporal element of Bataille's definition of sovereignty. Bataille regards as sovereign those who don't subordinate their present to the future, who "enjoy the present time without having anything else in view but this present time".[43] When we exist by the skin of our teeth, everything we do is in regard to our future. The working class is forced into a position of temporal servility, whereby nights of socialising with friends (or simply sleep) are replaced with caffeinated all-nighters of studying or work. When our lives are on the line, not a moment can be wasted. We have no choice but "to employ the present time for the sake of the future", a state of temporal servility wherein the idea of the future dominates our experience of the present.[44]

Is this temporal servility not a perfect description of what ambition does to our lives? Ambition ensures that our lives become things not to be lived in the present but subordinated to what they could be in the future. We are not what we're doing now but our goals and our earning potential. The sovereign position is to give up on ambition and everything it does.

As I've said what feels like a million times, ambition is an economic position adopted out of necessity rather than free and autonomous choice, and I'll freely admit I'm very lucky to be in the position I'm in. I'm comfortable enough that I can afford to waste some of my own time while others have to struggle much harder for much less in return. But the important thing to recognise is that life in a non-ambitious society wouldn't leave the sovereignty of aimlessness and wastefulness up to luck. Any society worth making would ensure people didn't have to subordinate themselves to a purpose or a life of productivity and thrift out of necessity. Sovereignty, as I've outlined in this chapter, is the name for the freedom a society like this would produce.

Sovereign Slackers: In Lieu of a Conclusion

A non-ambitious life, a sovereign life, is one free from the pressures of economic calculation and needing to be granted an aim or a purpose. Such a life might sound all too familiar to those who, like me, spent too much of their teens idolising the figures who made up the "slacker" archetype of the 1990s. Dante from *Clerks*, the Dude from *The Big Lebowski* and the guy from *Office Space* all lead lives of aimlessness and economic wastefulness, often putting themselves at odds with the people in their lives who want them to be a little more productive and to set their sights a little higher.

A notable thing about each of these slackers is that the question of money is almost entirely irrelevant to them. None of them are wealthy, but they don't appear to be struggling financially. The protagonist of *Office Space* doesn't hate his job because he's being exploited by his boss in the traditional Marxist sense but because filing paperwork is depressing and meaningless and because his boss is a dickhead who makes him work on weekends. Dante seems unhappy working at the convenience store in *Clerks* for the same reason I was unhappy working night shifts at a supermarket: out of a vague sense of social embarrassment more than anything else. The feeling that he should be living up to his potential, that he should want to be ambitious, is more of a motivation for Dante than money. As for the Dude, he's the only one who begins and ends his movie a happy man, and he's the only one for whom work isn't a concern. That the Dude misses his rent payments is brought up in the film, but one could infer that the struggle to pay his rent is more the result of his congenital laziness than of his living paycheck to paycheck. One could see him genuinely forgetting that he needs to pay it at all. Money is a non-issue for each of these characters, which suggests that, in an apparent paradox, being a slacker is something one must be able to afford.

This is why the complaint that slackers tend to be straight white men rubs me the wrong way. The statement itself is correct — all these protagonists *are* straight white men — but if we understand these movies as reflections of reality, we can see that it makes perfect sense that the people with the most social and economic privilege can afford to waste their money and go nowhere with their lives. Dante, the Dude and the *Office Space* guy slack off and reject the possibility of optimising their lives because they already live better lives than the majority of humanity. Their lives don't need improving. The same cannot be said for trans people abandoned by their families, for women relegated to thankless domestic servitude or for people of colour harassed by the police or suffering the consequences of colonialism. To paraphrase the sci-fi author William Gibson, slackerism is already here; it's just unevenly distributed.

The question remains, how do we respond to that uneven distribution? To my mind, there are two ways to respond to slackers being white men. The first is to point out that fact and say, "Why do these white men get away with not working and leeching off the rest of society? They should have to work just like the rest of us." Affects such as these have been labelled "negative solidarity", because while they're interested in everybody in society being on some kind of equal standing, what they actually call for is for levelling that playing field by *lowering* a group of people's standards of living and restricting our imaginations regarding how our lives could be different.[1] The other way to respond to slackerism's uneven distribution is to ask, "Why is it *only* white men who can afford to be aimless and waste all their human capital?" This second response recognises that slackerism is the privilege of a select few, but rather than taking that privilege away, it responds by calling for that privilege to be expanded to *everyone*.

The majority of people today, myself included, are encouraged to be economic maximisers, to find an aim for our lives and stick to it while being as productive as possible. We are supposed to dedicate our lives to building a career, a portfolio and vast sums of human capital, while we squirrel away as much as we can for less predictable times. Ambition springs from these conditions, and we thus assume that ambition is good as well as natural. The closest this book gets to a political vision is the communisation of slackerism: the idea that a non-ambitious life of aimlessness and economic wastefulness should no longer be limited to those who can afford it. This entails changing not only people's minds but also their living conditions. The only way to find out if ambition is really a "natural" inclination is to ensure that people don't need to be ambitious to survive. Let people live the lives of slackers, without needing to find a purpose or maximise their productivity, and we'll see just how natural ambition is.

Acknowledgements

As ever, first thanks go to my editor, Carl Neville at Repeater Books. His guidance has ensured that the book you're reading now is more coherent than the one I initially wrote. Many thanks also to the whole team at Repeater Books, as well as the recent departures, Josh Turner and Tariq Goddard, who will be missed. Since I don't have access to a university library system, thanks to the people who run and maintain *Library Genesis*, *Sci-Hub*, and the Facebook group "Ask for PDFs from People with Institutional Access". These have all become indispensable resources for me and show a better way of distributing and socialising knowledge. Lastly, I couldn't have written this without the encouragement and comments from my wife, Kate Seymour. Part-time work, home-making and writing make me infinitely happier than full-time work, and I couldn't live the life I do without her. She has always been my first reader, and lets me know when my laziness is getting the better of me.

Endnotes

Preface

1   Marx, K 1976, *Capital: Volume I*, trans. B Fowkes, Penguin, p. 718.
2   Niazi, A 2022, "Losing my Ambition", the *Cut*, https://www.thecut.com/2022/03/post-pandemic-loss-of-ambition.html, accessed 2 April 2024.
3   De Tocqueville, A 2010, *Democracy in America*, vol. 4, trans. JT Schleifer, Liberty Fund, Online Library of Liberty database, p. 1117.
4   Ibid., p. 1119.
5   Bridge, R 2016, *Ambition: Why it's Good to Want More and How to Get It*, Capstone, p. 4.
6   Jaquet, C 2023, *Transclasses: A Theory of Social Non-Reproduction*, trans. G Elliott, Verso, p. 24.

1. The Tyranny of Purpose

1   Cited in Foucault, M 1991, "Governmentality", in G Burchell, C Gordon & P Miller (eds), *The Foucault Effect: Studies in Governmentality*, University of Chicago Press, p. 93.
2   Aristotle 1999, *Nicomachean Ethics*, trans. T Irwin, 2nd edition, Hackett, p. 41.
3   Aristotle 1929, *The Physics*, trans. PH Wicksteed & FM Cornford, William Heinemann & Sons, Internet Archive, https://archive.org/details/in.ernet.dli.2015.183335/page/170/mode/2up?q=spiders%2C+ants, accessed 9 June 2024, p. 171.
4   Lucretius 2007, *The Nature of Things*, trans. AE Stallings,

Penguin, pp. 131–132.

5 *Capital: Volume I*, p. 284.

6 *Physics*, p. 175.

7 Tsao, T 2012, "The Tyranny of Purpose: Religion and Biotechnology in Ishiguro's *Never Let Me Go*", *Literature & Theology*, vol. 26, no. 2, pp. 214–232.

8 Ishiguro, K 2005, *Never Let Me Go*, Faber & Faber.

9 Cheung, K 2023, "Anti-Abortion Activist on 10-Year-Old Rape Victim: 'A Woman's Body Is Designed to Carry Life'", *Jezebel*, https://www.jezebel.com/anti-abortion-activist-on-10-year-old-rape-victim-a-w-1850354393, accessed 2 March 2024, emphasis added. For more detail on the 2022 rape case specifically, see Cheung, K 2022, "A 10-Year-Old Girl in Ohio Was Forced to Travel to Indiana for an Abortion", *Jezebel*, https://www.jezebel.com/a-10-year-old-girl-in-ohio-was-forced-to-travel-to-indi-1849136765, accessed 2 March 2024.

10 I'll also say that teleological thinking reduces men's role to reproduction and manual labour, but I think it goes without saying, and the inability or unwillingness of some cis women to have children led more smoothly to the issue of trans rights.

11 I'm not an expert on uterus implant surgeries, but there is reading available on the topic. See Samuel, L 2016, "With womb transplants a reality, transgender women dare to dream of pregnancies", *STAT*, https://www.statnews.com/2016/03/07/uterine-transplant-transgender/, accessed 19 February 2023. Australian Associated Press 2022, "'An amazing gift': Australia's first uterus transplants to take place in 2023", the *Guardian*, https://www.theguardian.com/society/2022/sep/09/an-amazing-gift-australias-first-uterus-transplants-to-take-place-in-2023, accessed 19 February 2023. Jones, BP *et al* 2021, "Perceptions and Motivations for Uterus Transplant in Transgender Women", *JAMA Network Open*, vol. 4, no. 1,

doi:10.1001/jamanetworkopen.2020.34561.

12 Fitzgerald, FS 1925, *The Great Gatsby*, Charles Scribner's Sons, p. 112.

13 Schürmann, R 1987, *Heidegger on Being and Acting: From Principles to Anarchy*, trans. C-M Gros, Indiana University Press.

14 Rose, N 1996, *Inventing Our Selves: Psychology, Power, and Personhood*, Cambridge University Press, p. 154.

15 Fitzgerald, FS 1990, *The Great Gatsby*, Penguin, p. 164.

16 *Inventing Our Selves*, p. 154.

2. Ambition and Capitalism

1 Jaquet, C 2023, *Transclasses: A Theory of Social non-reproduction*, trans. G Elliott, Verso, p. 23.

2 Guattari, F 2009, "Everybody wants to be a fascist", *Chaosophy: texts and interviews 1972–1977*, S Lotringer (ed.), trans. DL Sweet, J Becker, T Adkins, p 175.

3 *Capital, Volume I*, pp. 344–345.

4 *Mute Compulsion*, p. 319.

5 Read, J 2022, *The production of subjectivity: Marx and philosophy*, Brill, p. 132.

6 Aquinas, T 2017, *Summa Theologiae*, https://www.newadvent. org/summa/3131.htm, accessed 5 March 2023.

7 Cited in Herlihy, D 1973, "Three Patterns of Social Mobility in Medieval History", *Journal of Interdisciplinary History*, vol. 3, no. 4, p. 623.

8 2019, "An Homily Against Disobedience and Willful Rebellion", M Best & R Gaby (ed.), Internet Shakespeare Archive, https://internetshakespeare.uvic.ca/doc/Homilies_2–21_M/ complete/index.html accessed 26 February 2023.

9 Riser-Kositsky, S 2009, "The Political Intensification of Caste: India Under the Raj", *Penn. History Review*, vol. 17, no. 1, https://repository.upenn.edu/entities/publication/ed5a5971-

7b4e-4733-84e5-f254f3b3b421, accessed 1 September 2023.
Ahmad, I 1971, "Caste Mobility Movements in North India", *The Indian Economic & Social History Review*, vol. 8, no. 2, pp. 164–191.

10 Both these examples come from the historian Chris Dyer. See Musgrove, D 2020, "Social mobility in the Middle Ages: could medieval people improve their station?", *History Extra*, https://www.historyextra.com/period/medieval/people-social-mobility-middle-ages-peasants-serfs/, accessed 27 August 2023.

11 Carocci, S 2011, "Social mobility and the Middle Ages", *Continuity and Change*, vol. 26, no. 3, p. 385.

12 Ibid.

13 This is not to suggest that only the economic hierarchy exists under capitalism to the exclusion of race, gender, and geography, but I'm shining a light on capitalism's economic hierarchy of classes specifically.

14 Deleuze, G & Guattari, F 2009, *Anti-Oedipus: Capitalism and Schizophrenia*, trans. R Hurley, M Seem & HR Lane, Penguin Books, p. 254, emphasis in original.

15 The very Australian phenomenon of the "cashed-up bogan" is an instructive case here, as it indicates someone with lower-class mannerisms who nonetheless has large sums of money. See the cricketer Shane Warne and the media mogul Kerry Packer for examples.

16 *Transclasses*, p. 8.

17 Musgrove, D 2020, "Social mobility in the Middle Ages: could medieval people improve their station?", *History Extra*, https://www.historyextra.com/period/medieval/people-social-mobility-middle-ages-peasants-serfs/, accessed September 28 2022.

18 Stewart, H 2019, "Corbyn to drop social mobility as Labour goal in favour of opportunity for all", the *Guardian*, https://www.theguardian.com/politics/2019/jun/08/jeremy-corbyn-to-drop-

social-mobility-as-labour-goal, accessed 5 September 2023.

19 Althusser, L 2014, *On the Reproduction of Capitalism: Ideology and Ideological State Apparatuses*, trans. GM Goshgarian, Verso, p. 180.

20 Weber, M 2001, *The Protestant Ethic and the Spirit of Capitalism*, trans. T Parsons, Routledge.

21 Marx, K 2002, "Critique of Hegel's Philosophy of Right", *Marx on Religion*, J Raines (ed.), Temple University Press, p. 171.

22 "The Social Principles of Christianity", *Marx on Religion*, p. 185.

23 Marx and Weber are often pitted against each other on the basis that the former is "too materialist" for sociologists while the latter is "too idealist" for Marxists, but this strict dichotomy ignores what Marx and Weber actually believed. Marx wrote that "material force can only be overthrown by material force. But theory also becomes a material force once it has gripped the masses." In other words, ideas come to matter when taken up by a large enough number of people who act on those ideas. Conversely, Weber ends his study of the Protestant ethic on the note that material and economic forces are absolutely relevant to the developments of both capitalism *and* Protestantism itself, and that by analysing the cultural preconditions of capitalism, he by no means intended to suggest that material conditions were irrelevant. See "The Critique of Hegel's Philosophy of Right", *Marx on Religion*, p. 177 & *The Protestant Ethic and the Spirit of Capitalism*, p. 125.

24 Siegelbaum, LH 1988, *Stakhanovism and the politics of productivity in the USSR, 1935–1941*, Cambridge University Press, pp. 1–3.

25 Stalin, JV 2008, "Speech at the First All-Union Conference of Stakhanovites", *Marxists Internet Archive*, https://www.marxists.org/reference/archive/stalin/works/1935/11/17.htm, accessed 29 September 2022. Unfortunately, the translator of

this speech is not listed.

26 Tangentially, increased levels of consumerism also benefit the capitalist economy by expanding the economy. See Wolff, RD 2005, "Ideological State Apparatuses, Consumerism, and U.S. Capitalism: Lessons for the Left", *Rethinking Marxism*, vol. 17, no. 2, pp. 223–235.

27 Lordon, F 2014, *Willing Slaves of Capital: Spinoza & Marx on Desire*, trans. G Ash, Verso Books, pp. 28–31.

28 Ivanova, MN 2011, "Consumerism and the crisis: whither the 'American Dream'?", *Critical Sociology*, DOI: 10.1177/0896920510378770.

29 Steinbeck, J 2006, *Of Mice and Men*, Penguin, p. 86.

30 Wood, EM 2017, *The Origin of Capitalism: A Longer View*, Verso, pp. 86–87, emphasis added.

31 Minimising cost-of-living expenses is also why some American retirees flee to Vietnam, a country with a decent standard of living but considerably cheaper than the US. See Jennings, R 2019, "Americans are retiring to Vietnam, for cheap healthcare and a decent standard of living", *Los Angeles Times*, https://www.latimes.com/world-nation/story/2019-12-25/americans-are-retiring-to-vietnam-for-cheap-health-care-and-a-decent-living-standard, accessed 23 September 2023.

32 Santos, R 2022, "What Is 'Fuck You Money' and Do You Have Enough of It?", *VICE*, https://www.vice.com/en/article/xgdmg4/how-quit-job-early-invest-money-retire, accessed 23 September 2023.

33 Lordon, F 2014, *Willing Slaves of Capital: Spinoza & Marx on Desire*, trans. G Ash, Verso Books, p. 52.

34 Foucault, M 2008, *The History of Sexuality: Volume I: The Will to Knowledge*, trans. R Hurley, Penguin, pp. 88–89.

35 Marx, K 1973, *Grundrisse*, trans. M Nicolaus, Penguin, p. 241.

36 *The Birth of Biopolitics*, p. 226.

37 Boltanski, L & Chiapello, È 2018, *The New Spirit of Capitalism*, trans. G Elliott, Verso.

38 Marx, *Capital: Volume I*, p. 875.

39 *Capital: Volume I*, p. 899. My edition of *Capital*, like many others in English, translates the phrase to "silent compulsion", but I changed it to "mute" to relate more clearly to Mau's book.

40 Foucault, M 1982, "The Subject and Power", *Critical Inquiry*, vol. 8, no. 4, pp. 777–795.

41 Friedman, M 1951, "Neo-liberalism and its Prospects", *Hoover Institution Library*, https://miltonfriedman.hoover.org/internal/media/dispatcher/214957/full, accessed 29 May 2023.

42 Lordon, F 2014, *Willing Slaves of Capital: Spinoza & Marx on Desire*, trans. G Ash, Verso Books, p. 142.

43 Graeber, D 2019, *Bullshit Jobs: A Theory*, Penguin.

44 *Grundrisse*, p. 650.

45 Tairako, T 2019, "Marx on Peasants and Small-Scale Industry — The Changes of Marx's Insight Into The Pre-Capitalist Societies", *Hitotsubashi Journal of Social Studies*, vol. 50, no. 1, p. 18.

46 Spohrer, K, Stahl, G & Bowers-Brown, T 2017, "Constituting neoliberal subjects? 'Aspiration' as technology of government in UK policy discourse", *Journal of Education Policy*, DOI: 0.1080/02680939.2017.1336573.

3. Producing Ambitious Subjects: Or, How to Make Someone Want Something

1 Thatcher, M 1981, "Interview for *Sunday Times*", Margaret Thatcher Foundation Website, https://www.margaretthatcher.org/document/104475, accessed 8 June 2022.

2 Weiss, H 2019, *We Have Never Been Middle Class: How Social Mobility Misleads Us*, Verso, p. 64.

3 While I often quite like the work of Byung-Chul Han, his insistence that Foucault's power served a repressive, negative

function leaves a lot to be desired. See his chapters "Biopolitics" and "Foucault's Dilemma" in Han, B-C 2017, *Psychopolitics: Neoliberalism and New Technologies of Power*, trans. E Butler, Verso.

4   Foucault, M 2008, *The History of Sexuality: Volume I*, trans. R Hurley, Penguin, p. 136.

5   Foucault writes that "Discipline increases the forces of the body (in economic terms of utility) and diminishes these same forces (in political terms of obedience)." Foucault, M 1991, *Discipline and Punish: The Birth of the Prison*, trans. A Sheridan, Penguin, p. 138.

6   Foucault, M 1990, *The History of Sexuality, Volume I: An Introduction*, trans. R Hurley, Penguin, p. 61.

7   Foucault, M 1982, "The Subject and Power", *Critical inquiry*, vol. 8, no. 4, p. 781.

8   See, for example, a prominent English trade union advocating for fracking for the sake of creating and maintaining jobs. GMB Union 2022, "Fracking could create good jobs — but we must not repeat past mistakes, *GMB Union*, website, https://www.gmb.org.uk/news/fracking-could-create-good-jobs-we-must-not-repeat-past-mistakes, accessed 12 May 2023.

9   See Guattari, F & Negri, T 1990, *Communists Like Us: New Spaces of Liberty, New Lines of Alliance*, trans. M Ryan, Semiotext(e).

10   *Mute Compulsion*, p. 131.

11   *Capital: Volume I*, p. 899.

12   Read, J 2022, Read, J 2022, *The production of subjectivity: Marx and philosophy*, Brill, p. 4.

13   Feher, M 2009, "Self-Appreciation; or, the Aspirations of Human Capital", *Public Culture*, vol. 21, no. 1, p. 24.

14   Ibid., p. 30.

15   Ibid., p. 26, emphasis added.

16 *We Have Never Been Middle Class*, p. 96.

17 Koksal, I 2020, "The Rise of Online Learning", *Forbes*, https://www.forbes.com/sites/ilkerkoksal/2020/05/02/the-rise-of-online-learning/, accessed 10 October 2023.

18 *We Have Never Been Middle Class*, p. 107.

19 Ibid., p. 97.

20 Wood, EM 2017, *The Origin of Capitalism: A Longer View*, Verso, pp. 106–108.

21 *We Have Never Been Middle Class*, p. 97.

22 Horrocks, R 1997, *An Introduction to the Study of Sexuality*, Palgrave Macmillan, p. 68–70.

23 Ruti, M 2008, "The Fall of Fantasies: A Lacanian Reading of Lack, *Journal of the American Psychoanalytic Association*, vol. 56, no. 2, p. 484.

24 Ibid., p. 69.

25 Deleuze, G & Guattari, F 2009, *Anti-Oedipus: Capitalism and Schizophrenia*, trans. R Hurley, M Seem & HR Lane, Penguin Books, p. 25.

26 Even though Deleuze and Guattari harshly criticise Freud in *Anti-Oedipus* and *A Thousand Plateaus*, Freud was still quite radical compared to the psychoanalysis of his time. For example, Freud argued against the notion that sex was derived from a biological drive to reproduce and thus that the heteronormative couple represents the standard arborescent model which other sexual relationships can only imitate. See van Haute, P & Westerink, H 2016, "Introduction: Hysteria, Sexuality, and the Deconstruction of Normativity — Rereading Freud's 1905 Edition of *Three Essays on the Theory of Sexuality*", in P Van Haute & H Westerink (eds), *Three Essays on the Theory of Sexuality: The 1905 Edition*, Verso books, pp. xv–xxviii.

27 Deleuze, G & Guattari, F 2009, *Anti-Oedipus: Capitalism and*

Schizophrenia, trans. R Hurley, M Seem & HR Lane, Penguin Books, p. 28.

28 Ibid., p. 342.

29 Ibid., p. 191.

30 Clastres, P 1989, "Society Against the State", *Society Against the State: Essays in Political Anthropology*, trans. R Hurley, Zone Books, pp. 189–218.

31 Ibid., p. 190, emphases added.

32 Ibid.

33 *Capital: Volume I*, p. 876.

34 Ibid., p. 881.

35 Federici, S 2021, *Caliban and the Witch: Women, the Body and Primitive Accumulation*, Penguin.

36 Ibid., p. 19.

37 Ibid., p. 78.

38 One could argue that the lack which primitive accumulation imposed on women, the lack of social agency, the subordination to men of an equal social position, their sequestration in the reproductive domestic sphere rather than the productive workforce, is the origin of the kind of liberal "Lean In" feminism which posits that succeeding in the corporate and professional world is the solution to women's problems. In fact, the author of *Lean In*, Sheryl Sandberg, argues that a significant cause of women's lack of social stature is an "ambition gap" between women and men. See Foster, D 2016, *Lean Out*, Repeater Books.

39 Thompson, C 1943, "'Penis Envy' in Women", *Psychiatry*, vol. 6, no. 2, pp. 123–125.

40 For information on this, see Smith, R 2022, "Almost one-in-10 Australian homes were 'vacant' on Census night", *News. com.au*, https://www.news.com.au/finance/money/investing/

almost-onein10-australian-homes-were-vacant-on-census-night/news-story/e5da221268ad7331c2882a4feefd0db1, accessed 7 April 2023. For an analysis of the *reasons* for vacant housing from a website for real estate investors, see Mata, M 2017, "Why are so many homes being left vacant by owners?", *Your Investment Property*, https://www.yourinvestment-propertymag.com.au/news/why-are-so-many-homes-being-left-vacant-by-owners, accessed 7 April 2023.

41 Giles, DB 2021, *A Mass Conspiracy To Feed People: Food Not Bombs and the World-Class Waste of Global Cities*, Duke University Press, p. 5.

42 Ibid., p. 30.

43 *Anti-Oedipus*, p. 28.

44 Marx, K 1978, "Economic and Philosophic Manuscripts of 1844", *The Marx-Engels Reader*, 2nd Edition, R Tucker (ed.), WW Norton and Company, pp. 66–125.

45 Dupré, L 1972, "Hegel's concept of alienation and Marx's reinterpretation of it", *Hegel-Studien*, vol. 7, pp. 217–236.

46 "Economic and Philosophic Manuscripts of 1844", p. 79.

47 Ariely, D, Kamenica, E & Prelec, D 2008, "Man's search for meaning: the case of Legos", *Journal of Economic Behaviour and Organisation*, vol. 67, pp. 671–677.

48 Since Althusser's anti-humanism and his idea of the "epistemological break" between the early and late Marx, Marx's concept of alienation has largely been abandoned. Even though I rely much more on Marx's later works, I consider the concept of alienation to be one more of Marx's critical tools.

49 "Economic and Philosophic Manuscripts of 1844", p. 72.

50 Baking during COVID has been analysed to death, but for a short range of perspectives, see Young, J 2021, "A Return to Tradition: The Significance of Baking During COVID-19', *Digest*, vol. 8, no. 1/2, pp. 43–65, Gammon, K 2020, "Kneading

to relax? How coronavirus prompted a surge in stress baking", the *Guardian*, https://www.theguardian.com/us-news/2020/apr/19/coronavirus-stress-baking-sourdough-kneading-relax, accessed 30 September 2023, St James, E 2020, "How to bake bread", *Vox*, https://www.vox.com/the-highlight/2020/5/19/21221008/how-to-bake-bread-pandemic-yeast-flour-baking-ken-forkish-claire-saffitz, accessed 30 September 2023.

51 2012, *Night of Too Many Stars*, Comedy Central.

52 "Economic and Philosophic Manuscripts of 1844", p. 72.

53 *Transclasses*, p. 24.

54 Hillman, J 1996, *The Soul's Code: In Search of Character and Calling*, Random House Australia, p. 159.

55 Ibid.

56 This is supposed to flip the motivational-model relationship upside-down, saying that the contents of our souls are the archetype for the people who we listen to on earth, who are the copies. But for all its supposed innovation in the flipping of this relation, its results are the same, as Hillman basically says we need motivational figures on whom to model a portion of our lives.

57 *Transclasses*, pp. 25–26.

58 Australian Institute of Sport 2022, *Australian Institute of Sport*, website, https://www.ais.gov.au/media-centre/news/aussie-athletes-set-to-inspire-school-kids-across-the-country, accessed 4 October 2023.

59 This may not be the only reason for the name of Tate's program to change, but his "The Real World" is specifically constructed against "the Matrix", a term currently in vogue among the online right.

60 Magee, C 2023, "I went inside Andrew Tate's Hustler University — where 'Gs' celebrate making $11", the *Independent*, https://www.independent.co.uk/news/world/europe/

andrew-tate-news-hustler-university-prison-b2270271.html, accessed 7 October 2023.

61 Franklin, B 1748, "Advice to a Young Tradesman, Written By an Old One", *Founders Online*, archive, https://founders. archives.gov/documents/Franklin/01-03-02-0130, accessed 7 October 2023.

62 *Transclasses*, pp. 55–56.

63 Ibid., p. 55.

4. On Failure

1 Han, B-C 2015, *The Burnout Society*, trans. E Butler, Stanford University Press, p. 9.

2 I took the example of a photocopier from Wike, VS & Showler, RL 2010, "Kant's Concept of the Highest Good and the Archetype-Ectype Distinction", *The Journal of Value Inquiry*, vol. 44, no. 4, p. 527, doi: 10.1007/s10790-010-9252-y. The authors describe the differences between the archetype and ectype, original and copy, as "blemishes" of the latter, which I'm not a fan of for reasons stated in the text.

3 Scott, S 2023, "Failed Identities: On the Processes and Meanings of Unformed Alternate Selves", in A Mica, M Pawlak, A Horolets & P Kubicki (eds), *Routledge International Handbook of Failure*, Taylor & Francis, p. 112.

4 Ibid., p. 114.

5 Spohrer, K 2018, "The problem with 'raising aspiration' strategies: social mobility requires more than personal ambitions", *London School of Economic and Political Science*, blog post, https://blogs.lse.ac.uk/politicsandpolicy/raising-aspiration-government-strategy/, accessed 24 January 2024.

6 Contrary to similar stories based in the US and UK, in the Australian context, where one goes to high school has a greater impact on social and cultural capital than where one goes to

university.

7   Tsiolkas, C 2015, *Barracuda*, Allen & Unwin, p. 22.

8   Ibid., p. 88. For those unfamiliar, "Macca's" is the Australian slang term for McDonald's.

9   Cited in Blumenfeld, J 2018, *All Things Are Nothing To Me: The Unique Philosophy of Max Stirner*, Zer0 Books.

10 Stirner, M 2017, *The Unique and Its Property*, trans. W Land-streicher, Underworld Amusements, p. 62.

11 Bacon, F [n.d.], "Of Ambition", *Essays of Francis Bacon*, http://www.authorama.com/essays-of-francis-bacon-37.html, accessed 12 November 2022.

12 Liu, W 2020, *Abolish Silicon Valley: how to liberate technology from capitalism*, Repeater Books.

13 Ibid., p. 35.

14 Ibid., p. 57.

15 Iluri, S 2020, "The AI (Artificial Intelligence) Supervisor is the Future of Work", *Linkedin*, blog post, https://www.linkedin.com/pulse/ai-artificial-intelligence-supervisor-future-work-satya-iluri, accessed 29 January 2024; Markow, W 2023, "Why Artificial Intelligence Will Make Tech Workers More Human", *Forbes*, https://www.forbes.com/sites/forbestechcouncil/2023/05/05/why-artificial-intelligence-will-make-tech-workers-more-human/?sh=2d9bb4e549b4, accessed 29 January 2024; Jarrahi, MH, Monahan, K & Leonardi, P 2023, "What Will Working with AI Really Require?", *Harvard Business Review*, https://hbr.org/2023/06/what-will-working-with-ai-really-require, accessed 29 January 2024.

16 It's been noted by analysts of neoliberalism that the ability of applicants to adapt is more important to potential employers than the particular skills they might have. For example, Boltanski and Chiapello write that "since projects are by their very nature temporary, the ability to disengage from a project

in order to be *available* for new connections counts as much as the capacity for engagement […]. Far from being attached to an occupation or clinging to a qualification, the great man [in neoliberalism] proves *adaptable* and *flexible*, able to switch from one situation to a very different one, and adjust to it […]. It is precisely this *adaptability* and *versatility* that make him employable." But we should recognise that these authors are almost always referring to those in careers most like theirs: white-collar professionals. It's much more conceivable, for example, that one can move from being a policy writer for environmental legislation to working as an environmental consultant for a mining company than for someone to move from being an electrician to a history teacher. The white-collar professional jobs associated with so-called "cognitive capitalism" remain the minority around the world. Boltanski, L & Chiapello, È 2018, trans. G Elliott, Verso, p. 112. And though we might associate "deskilling" with jobs in manufacturing, with its history of the Fordist assembly line, labour journalism covering television and film writers shows that even the "creative industries" are not immune to deskilling. See Press, A 2023, "Hollywood is on Strike Against High-Tech Exploitation", *Jacobin*, https://jacobin.com/2023/07/hollywood-writers-actors-strike-studios-streaming, accessed 21 August 2023.

17 *Capital: Volume I*, p. 549.

18 Spinoza, BD 1996, *Ethics*, trans. E Curley, Penguin, p. 81. See also Fisher, M 2015, "Abandon hope (summer is coming)", *k-punk*, blog post, http://k-punk.org/abandon-hope-summer-is-coming/, accessed 21 August 2023.

19 *Barracuda*, p. 216.

20 Radiohead 2007, *In Rainbows*.

21 Pareles, J 2007, "Pay What You Want For This Article", *New York Times*, https://www.nytimes.com/2007/12/09/arts/music/09pare.

html?ex=1354856400&en=ec2f1c29937292be&ei=5090&part-ner=rssuserland&emc=rss&pagewanted=all, accessed 10 November 2022.

22 Adams, T 2013, "Thom Yorke: 'If I can't enjoy this now, when do I start?'", the *Guardian*, https://www.theguardian.com/music/2013/feb/23/thom-yorke-radiohead-interview, accessed 11 November 2022.

23 "Under free competition, the immanent laws of capitalist production confront the individual capitalist as a coercive force external to him." Ibid., p. 381.

24 *Capital: Volume I*, p. 739, emphasis added.

25 Marx, K & Engels, F 2010, *The Communist Manifesto*, Penguin Books, p. 237.

26 Foucault, M 1982, "The Subject and Power", *Critical Inquiry*, vol. 8, no. 4, trans. L Sawyer, p. 789.

27 Mau, M 2023, *Mute Compulsion: A Marxist Theory of the Economic Power of Capital*, Verso, p. 211.

28 Ibid.

29 Marx makes this clear in the first volume of *Capital*, on why capitalists don't get more money just hoarding it. "The exclusion of money from circulation would constitute precisely the opposite of its valorization as capital." Marx, K 1976, *Capital: Volume I*, trans. B Fowkes, Penguin, p. 735.

30 Ibid., p. 711, emphasis added.

31 A recent book on this subject is Edmondson, A 2023, *Right Kind of Wrong: The Science of Failing Well*, Simon & Schuster. For a freely available article by that book's author, see Edmondson, AC 2011, "Strategies of Learning From Failure", *Harvard Business Review*, https://hbr.org/2011/04/strategies-for-learning-from-failure, accessed 22 January 2024.

32 Jacobs, K & Malpas, J 2023, "Politics, Sociology, and the 'Inevitability' of Failure", in A Mica, M Pawlak, A Horolets &

P Kubicki (eds), *Routledge International Handbook of Failure*, Taylor & Francis, pp. 423–432.

33 Bruns, GL 2011, *On Ceasing to be Human*, Stanford University Press, p. 59.

34 Foucault, M 1982, "The Subject and Power", *Critical Inquiry*, vol. 8, no. 4, p. 785.

35 Freud, "Mourning and Melancholia", *The Standard Edition of the Complete Psychological Works of Sigmund Freud: Volume XIV (1914–1916)*, The Hogarth Press, p. 244.

36 Cited in Bruns, GL 2011, *On Ceasing to be Human*, Stanford University Press, p. 58.

37 For more on the inexpressibility and unshareability of pain, see Scarry, E 1985, *The Body in Pain: the making and unmaking of the world*, Oxford University Press.

38 I credit this idea to Rohan Bastin, an anthropology professor I had during my undergrad days. For an assessment of self-injury as an artistic practice, see Brucher, R 2019, "Self-Injuring Body Art: Strategies of De/Subjectivation", *New German Critique*, vol. 46, no. 2, pp. 151–170.

39 Bayat, A 2010, *Life as Politics: How Ordinary People Change the Middle East*, Amsterdam University Press, p. 14.

40 Ibid., p. 20. This phrase is italicised in the text, but I removed it for the sake of readability.

41 Thompson, EP 1966, *The making of the English working class*, Vintage Books, p. 9.

42 Marx, K & Engels, F 2010, *The Communist Manifesto*, Penguin, p. 233.

43 Evans, D 2023, *A Nation of Shopkeepers: The Unstoppable Rise of the Petty Bourgeoisie*, Repeater Books, p. 52.

5. Radical Ambitions?

1 Connolly, J 1907, "We Only Want the Earth", *Songs of Freedom*,

Marxists Internet Archive, https://www.marxists.org/archive/connolly/1907/xx/wewnerth.htm, accessed 21 March 2024.

2   Nietzsche, F 1989, *On the Genealogy of Morals and Ecce Homo*, trans. W Kaufmann & RJ Hollingdale, Vintage books, pp. 217–218.

3   Montaigne, M "Of Managing the Will", *Essays of Michel de Montaigne*, trans. C Cotton, WC Hazlitt (ed.), Project Gutenberg Archive, https://www.gutenberg.org/files/3600/3600-h/3600-h.htm.

4   Sorel, G 1999, *Reflections on Violence*, trans. TE Hulme & J Jennings, Cambridge University Press, p. 43.

5   Benjamin, W 2004, "Critique of Violence" *One-Way Street and other writings*, trans. E Jephcott & K Shorter, Verso, pp. 147–175.

6   Sorel says explicitly in the introduction to his *Reflections on Violence* that his task is to "enquire into the function of *the violence of the working classes* in contemporary socialism". *Reflections on Violence*, p. 42.

7   Benjamin calls these two forms of violence "mythic violence" and "divine violence" respectively, but I've chosen to set aside the more theological implications of Benjamin's essay because they're not strictly relevant here.

8   Benjamin, "Critique of Violence", p. 171.

9   Georges Sorel, cited in Benjamin, "Critique of Violence", p. 164.

10 Benjamin, "Critique of Violence", pp. 164–165, emphasis added.

11 Timofeeva, O 2022, *Solar Politics*, Polity, p. 41.

12 Benjamin, "Critique of Violence", p. 175.

13 Agamben, G 2014, "For a theory of destituent power", *Critical Legal Thinking*, accessed 20 August 2022, https://criticallegalthinking.com/2014/02/05/theory-destituent-power/. Emphasis added.

14 The Invisible Committee 2017, *Now*, trans. R Hurley, Semiotext(e), p. 78.

15 The Invisible Committee 2015, *To Our Friends*, trans. R Hurley, Semiotext(e), p. 75.

16 Ibid., p. 81.

17 I'm referring to the YouTube channels PragerU and Bari Weiss's University of Austin.

18 For an in-depth example of this specific critique of the university, see the chapter "The University and the Undercommons" in Harney, S & Moten, F 2013, *The Undercommons: Fugitive Planning & Black Study*, Minor Compositions.

19 Lawrence, TE 2014, "Guerrilla Warfare", *Encyclopaedia Britannica*, https://www.britannica.com/topic/T-E-Lawrence-on-guerrilla-warfare-1984900, accessed 10 March 2023.

20 Ibid.

21 Ibid.

22 *Now*, p. 83.

23 Bacon, F [n.d.], "Of Ambition", *Essays of Francis Bacon*, http://www.authorama.com/essays-of-francis-bacon-37.html, accessed 12 November 2022.

24 Even though I'm choosing to draw from Bacon's understanding of the events, like much of Roman history, this conflict is fairly contested by both ancient and contemporary historians, and I'm by no means equipped to enter that debate.

25 Forgey, Q 2020, "AOC: 'In any other country, Joe Biden and I would not be in the same party'", *Politico*, https://www.politico.com/news/2020/01/06/alexandria-ocasio-cortez-joe-biden-not-same-party-094642, accessed 15 March 2024.

26 Robin, C 2018, "Ocasio-Cortez, the Left, and the Future of Palestine", *Jacobin*, https://jacobin.com/2018/07/alexandria-ocasio-cortez-israel-palestine-occupation, accessed 22 March 2024.

27 Uddin, R 2021, "AOC faces backlash for crying, but not voting, over bill to fund Israel's Iron Dome", *Middle East Eye*, https://

www.middleeasteye.net/news/israel-iron-dome-alexandria-oc-asio-cortez-aoc-present-condemned, accessed 22 March 2024.

28 Kaminkow, R 2023, "Railroad Workers United: 'We Would Never Concede Our Right to Strike'", *Jacobin*, https://jacobin.com/2023/04/railroad-workers-united-aoc-strike-vote-rank-and-file, accessed 15 March 2024.

29 Villarreal, A 2021, "'Medium is the message': AOC defends 'tax the rich' dress worn to Met Gala", the *Guardian*, https://www.theguardian.com/us-news/2021/sep/14/aoc-defends-tax-the-rich-dress-met-gala, accessed 15 March 2024.

30 DeBoer, F 2023, "AOC is Just a Regular Old Democrat Now", *New York Magazine*, https://nymag.com/intelligencer/2023/07/alexandria-ocasio-cortez-is-just-a-regular-old-democrat-now.html, accessed 15 March 2024.

31 Lenin, VI 1999, *State and Revolution: the Marxist Theory of the State & the Tasks of the Proletariat in the Revolution*, trans. Zodiac & B Baggins, Marxists Internet Archive, https://www.marxists.org/archive/lenin/works/1917/staterev/, accessed 17 March 2024.

32 Political philosopher Michael LeBuffe convincingly relates the state's perseverance to Spinoza's idea of "conatus", or the will to perseverance. See LeBuffe, M 2021, "Citizens and States in Spinoza's *Political Treatise*", *Mind*, vol. 130, no. 519, pp. 809–832.

33 Shlapentokh, DV 1996, "Revolutionary as a Career", *Communist and Post-Communist Studies*, vol. 29, no. 3, pp. 331–361.

34 Graeber, D 2018, *Bullshit Jobs: the Rise of Pointless Work and What We Can Do About It*, Penguin.

35 Lenin, VI 1972, "The Taylor System — Man's Enslavement by the Machine", trans. B Isaacs & J Fineberg, Marxists Internet Archive, https://www.marxists.org/archive/lenin/works/1914/mar/13.htm, accessed 17 March 2024. See also Devinatz, VG 2003, "Lenin as Scientific Manager Under Monopoly Capital-

ism, State Capitalism, and Socialism, a Response to Scoville", *Industrial Relations*, vol. 42, no. 3, pp. 513–520.

36 Ibid.

37 *Now*, p. 85.

38 Cited in Newman, S 2016, "What is an Insurrection?: Destituent Power and Ontological Anarchy in Agamben and Stirner", *Political Studies*, DOI: 10.1177/0032321716654498.

39 Marx, K 1978, "Economic and Philosophic Manuscripts of 1844", in RC Tucker (ed.), *The Marx-Engels Reader*, 2nd edition, WW Norton & Company, p. 84.

40 Marx, K 1978, "The British Rule in India", in RC Tucker (ed.), *The Marx-Engels Reader*, 2nd edition, WW Norton & Company, p. 658.

41 Ibid.

42 Marx, K & Engels, F 1998, *The German Ideology*, unnamed translator, Prometheus Books, p. 57, emphasis original.

43 Engels, F 1967, "The Principles of Communism", *Selected Works: Volume I*, trans. P Sweezy, Marxists Internet Archive, https://www.marxists.org/archive/marx/works/1847/11/princom.htm, accessed 7 March 2024.

44 *Capital: Volume I*, p. 929. See also Blumenfeld, J 2023, "Expropriation of the expropriators", *Philosophy & Social Criticism*, vol. 49, no. 4, DOI: 10.1177/01914537211059513.

45 Marx, K & Engels, F 2022, *The German Ideology: a new abridgement*, Repeater Books, p. 54.

46 Ibid.

47 Noys, B 2012, *Communization and its Discontents: Contestation, Critique, and Contemporary Struggles*, Minor Compositions.

48 The Invisible Committee 2009, *The Coming Insurrection*, Semiotext(e), p. 16.

49 Guattari, F & Negri, T 1990, *Communists Like Us: New Spaces of Liberty, New Lines of Alliance*, trans. M Ryan, Semiotext(e), p. 10.

50 Tarì, M 2021, *There is no unhappy revolution: the communism of destitution*, trans. R Braude, Common Notions, p. 74, emphasis original.

51 It was a minor scandal on the left when Søren Mau, the author of the universally well-received book *Mute Compulsion*, recently outlined a model for communism on the blog for Verso. Even those who would praise *Mute Compulsion* for its keen analysis of capitalism couldn't help but be disappointed when reading Mau's vision for a communist society. See Mau, S 2023, "Communism is Freedom", *Verso*, blog post, https://www.versobooks.com/en-gb/blogs/news/communism-is-freedom, accessed 7 March 2024. See also Neel, PA & Chavez, N [no date], "Forest and Factory: the Science and the Fiction of Communism", *Endnotes*, https://endnotes.org.uk/posts/forest-and-factory, accessed 7 March 2024.

52 Agamben, G 2023, "Destituent Potentiality and the Critique of Realization", trans. K Attell, *South Atlantic Quarterly*, vol. 122, no. 1, p. 10.

53 Tarì, M 2021, *There is no unhappy revolution: the communism of destitution*, trans. R Braude, Common Notions, p. 20.

54 Ibid., pp. 18–19.

55 Jaquet, C 2023, *Transclasses: A Theory of Social Non-Reproduction*, trans. G Elliott, Verso, p. 24.

6. The World Against Ambition

1 p. 76.

2 Caprino, K 11, "Busting the Myth That Women Aren't As Ambitious as Men", *Forbes*, https://www.forbes.com/sites/kathycaprino/2011/11/28/busting-the-myth-that-women-arent-as-ambitious-as-men/?sh=3827db3767da, accessed 14 May 2024.

3 Hsu, A 2023, "Women are earning more money. But they're still picking up a heavier load at home", *NPR*, https://www.npr.

org/2023/04/13/1168961388/pew-earnings-gender-wage-gap-housework-chores-child-care, accessed 14 May 2024.

4   Foster, D 2015, *Lean Out*, Repeater Books. See in particular Chapter 5.

5   Abadi, P 2013, "Margaret Thatcher: The Glass-Ceiling Shatterer Who Thought Feminism Was 'Poison'", *Ms. Magazine*, https://msmagazine.com/2013/04/09/margaret-thatcher-the-glass-ceiling-shatterer-who-thought-feminism-was-poison/, accessed 18 May 2024.

6   *Lean Out*, pp. 52–53.

7   Ibid., p. 54.

8   Shriver, L 2013, "Muscular Feminism", *Slate*, https://slate.com/human-interest/2013/04/margaret-thatcher-was-a-real-feminist.html, accessed 18 May 2024.

9   Cited in Abadi 2013, "Margaret Thatcher: The Glass-Ceiling Shatterer Who Thought Feminism Was 'Poison'".

10 Fahadi, PR 2024, "'The Man': Taylor's feminism could go so much further", *Pursuit*, University of Melbourne blog, https://pursuit.unimelb.edu.au/articles/the-man-taylor-s-feminism-could-go-so-much-further, accessed 20 May 2024.

11 Gottesman, T 2016, "EXCLUSIVE: Beyoncé Wants to Change the Conversation", *Elle*, https://www.elle.com/fashion/a35286/beyonce-elle-cover-photos/, accessed 26 May 2024.

12 Kale, S 2016, "How Much It Sucks to Be a Sri Lankan Worker Making Beyoncé's New Clothing Line", *Vice*, https://www.vice.com/en/article/d7anay/beyonce-topshop-ivy-park-sweatshop-factory-labor, accessed 26 May 2024.

13 An opinion piece for the *Guardian* says just that. See Slater, S 2016, "Don't blame Beyoncé for the harsh lives of garment makers", the *Guardian*, https://www.theguardian.com/commentisfree/2016/may/18/beyonce-ivy-park-harsh-lives-garment-makers-fashion-branding-consumers, accessed 26 May 2024.

14 Cited in Bottici, C 2022, *Anarchafeminism*, Bloomsbury, p. 5.

15 I'm aware that there have been many critiques of making a clear distinction between reproductive and productive labour, but consider my use of the distinction a heuristic device for the sake of this chapter.

16 Barca, S 2020, *Forces of Reproduction: Notes for a Counter-Hegemonic Anthropocene*, Cambridge University Press, p. 1.

17 *Caliban and the Witch*, p. 19, emphasis added.

18 Federici, S 2004, *Caliban and the Witch: Women, the Body and Primitive Accumulation*, Penguin, p. 78.

19 Marx, K 1973, *Grundrisse*, trans. M Nicolaus, Penguin, p. 488.

20 *Capital: Volume I*, p. 132.

21 Conan O'Brien 2021, "Conan & Norm Macdonald Cook With Gordon Ramsay | Late Night with Conan O'Brien", YouTube video, https://www.youtube.com/watch?v=KdOXM3I_5hk, accessed 1 June 2024.

22 Morgan, Z 2018, "Why are our professional kitchens still male dominated?", *BBC*, https://www.bbc.com/news/uk-wales-45486646, accessed 1 June 2024.

23 Mauss, M 1990, *The Gift: the form and reason for exchange in archaic societies*, Routledge.

24 *Capital: Volume I*, p. 128.

25 Mies, M 1998, *Patriarchy and Accumulation on a World Scale: Women in the International Division of Labour*, Zed Books, p. 45.

26 Cited in Horgan, A 2021, *Lost in Work: Escaping Capitalism*, Pluto Press, p. 39

27 *Capital: Volume I*, p. 131.

28 Chini, M 2024, "Europe's last ancient forests being cut down for IKEA furniture, report shows", the *Brussels Times*, https://www.brusselstimes.com/1000082/europes-last-ancient-forests-being-cut-down-for-ikea-furniture-report-shows, accessed 26 May 2024.

29 *Ecofeminism as Politics*, p. 58.

30 *Ecofeminism as Politics*, p. 93.

31 This is why some take issue with the term reproductive labour to begin with, because it implies it's secondary to productive labour, when in fact the opposite is true. See ibid., p. 95.

32 Eco-Marxists often refer to this separation as the "metabolic rift", but I chose not to use that term because it would require a larger exploration than is relevant here. For more writing on the metabolic rift, see Saito, K 2022, *Marx in the Anthropocene: Towards the Idea of Degrowth Communism*, Cambridge University Press, p. 24.

33 *Capital: Volume I*, p. 637.

34 *Marx in the Anthropocene*, pp. 32–32.

35 Coren, MJ 2023, "Why you should buy clothes to last (almost) forever", the *Washington Post*, https://www.washingtonpost.com/climate-environment/2023/11/07/long-lasting-clothes-fast-fashion/, accessed 29 May 2024.

36 Cited in Beyond Plastic 2023, "What's the problem with fast fashion?", *PIRG*, https://pirg.org/articles/whats-the-problem-with-fast-fashion/, accessed 24 May 2024,

37 Maiti, R 2024, "Fast Fashion and Its Environmental Impact", *Earth.org*, https://earth.org/fast-fashions-detrimental-effect-on-the-environment/, accessed 29 May 2024.

38 Mull, A 2023, "The Instant Pot Failed Because It Was a Good Product", the *Atlantic*, https://www.theatlantic.com/technology/archive/2023/06/instant-pot-bankrupt-private-equity/674414/, accessed 21 May 2024.

39 *Marx in the Anthropocene*, p. 29.

40 Li, Z 2021, "The Environmental Impacts on the Reversal of the Chicago River", blog op-ed, *University of Chicago*, https://voices.uchicago.edu/findingchicago/2021/08/27/the-environmental-impacts-on-the-reversal-of-the-chicago-river/, accessed 27

May 2024.

41 Huseynli, O 2024, "Unleashing the Power of Cloud Seeding: Navigating Potentials and Pitfalls", *Earth.org*, https://earth.org/unleashing-the-power-of-cloud-seeding-navigating-potential-and-pitfalls/, accessed 27 May 2024.

42 *Marx in the Anthropocene*, p. 111.

43 Phillips, L 2019, "The degrowth delusion", *Open Democracy*, https://www.opendemocracy.net/en/oureconomy/degrowth-delusion/, accessed 22 June 2023.

44 *Marx in the Anthropocene*, p. 123.

45 *Ecofeminism as Politics*, pp. 38–39.

46 Asafu-Adjaye, J, Brook, B, Blomqvist, L, Defries, R, Brand, S, Ellis, E, Foreman, C, Lynas, M, Keith, D, Nordhaus, T, Lewis, M, Pielke, R Jr, Pritzker, R, Shellenberger, M, Roy, J, Stone, R, Sagoff, M & Teague, P 2015, *An Ecomodernist Manifesto*, http://www.ecomodernism.org/, accessed 22 June 2023, p. 6

47 Salleh, A 1997, *Ecofeminism as Politics: nature, Marx and the postmodern*, Zed Books, p. 13.

48 See in particular Ariel Salleh's *Ecofeminism as Politics* and Stefania Barca's *Forces of Reproduction*.

49 Saito, K 2022, *Marx in the Anthropocene: Towards the idea of degrowth communism*, Cambridge University Press. I'm not the first person to bring up synergies between ecofeminism and degrowth. See Barca, S et al., 2023, "Caring Communities for Radical Change: What Can Feminist Political Ecology Bring to Degrowth?", in Harcourt et al (eds), *Contours of Feminist Political Ecology*, Palgrave, pp. 177–206. See also Dengler, C & Lang, M 2021, "Commoning Care: Feminist Degrowth Visions for a Socio-Ecological Transformation", *Feminist Economics*, vol. 28, no. 1, pp. 1–28.

50 Turhan, E & Barca, S 2022, "Keeping the world alive and healthy: The radical realism of the 'forces of reproduc-

tion' — An interview with Stefania Barca", *resilience*, https://www.resilience.org/stories/2022-02-07/keeping-the-world-alive-and-healthy-the-radical-realism-of-the-forces-of-reproduction-an-interview-with-stefania-barca/, accessed 25 June 2023. See also Barca, S 2020, *Forces of Reproduction: Notes for a Counter-Hegemonic Anthropocene*, Cambridge University Press, p. 28.

51 Marx, K 1973, *Grundrisse*, trans. M Nicolaus, Penguin, p. 488; Marx, K 1981, *Capital: Volume 3*, trans. D Fernbach, Penguin, p. 970, emphasis added. The passage this quote comes from describes the system of reproduction and production in societies Marx describes as "primitive communism", but I think it fits as a way to describe the communism system of reproduction and production.

7. Wasting Our Potential

1 Johnson, S 1758, "No. 1. The Idler's Character", *Samuel Johnson's Essays*, https://www.johnsonessays.com/the-idler/no-1-the-idlers-character/, accessed 23 April 2024.

2 Popova, M 2012, "Kurt Vonnegut's 8 Tips on How to Write a Great Story", the *Atlantic*, https://www.theatlantic.com/entertainment/archive/2012/04/kurt-vonneguts-8-tips-on-how-to-write-a-great-story/255401/, accessed 28 April 2024.

3 Lutz, T 2021, *Aimlessness*, Columbia University Press, pp. 75–77.

4 Ibid., p. 76.

5 Melville, H 2012, *Moby-Dick*, Penguin, p. 85.

6 Ibid., pp. 5–6.

7 Ibid., p. 88.

8 Ibid., p. 197.

9 Ibid., p. 196.

10 "God help thee, old man, thy thoughts have created a creature in thee; and he whose intense thinking thus makes him a Pro-

metheus; a vulture feeds upon that heart for ever; that vulture the very creature he creates." Ibid., p. 236.

11 See Lordon's *Willing Slaves of Capital* for more on employees subordinating their desires to those of their boss. Lordon, F 2014, *Willing Slaves of Capital: Spinoza & Marx on Desire*, trans. G Ash, Verso Books.

12 Ibid., p. 247.

13 Ibid., p. 191.

14 Ibid., pp. 550–551.

15 Ibid., p. 662.

16 Shelley, PB 1977, "Ozymandias", *Shelley's Poetry and Prose*, archived in Poetry Foundation, https://www.poetryfoundation.org/poems/46565/ozymandias, accessed 5 May 2024.

17 Cited in Branch, WG 1997, "Introduction", in WG Branch (ed.), *Herman Melville: The Critical Heritage*, Routledge, p. 27.

18 Ibid.

19 Ibid., p. 28.

20 Yeung, P 2019, "The Toxic Effects of Electronic Waste in Accra, Ghana", *Bloomberg*, https://www.bloomberg.com/news/articles/2019-05-29/the-rich-world-s-electronic-waste-dumped-in-ghana, accessed 5 May 2024.

21 Bataille, G 1989, *The Accursed Share: Volume I: Consumption*, trans. R Hurley, Zone Books, p. 23.

22 *The Accursed Share: Volume II & Volume III: The History of Eroticism & Sovereignty*, trans. R Hurley, Zone Books, p. 230.

23 *The Accursed Share: Volume I*, p. 10.

24 Sharpe, LL 2005, "Play does not enhance social cohesion in a cooperative mammal", *Animal Behaviour*, vol. 70, pp. 551–558.

25 Sharpe, LL & Cherry, MI 2003, "Social play does not reduce aggression in wild meerkats", *Animal Behaviour*, vol. 66, no. 5,

pp. 989–997.

26 Caro, TM 1980, "Effects of the Mother, Object Play, and Adult Experience on Predation in Cats", *Behavioral and Neural Biology*, vol. 29, pp. 29–51.

27 *The Accursed Share: Volumes 2 & 3*, p. 198.

28 Ibid., p. 280.

29 Mok, A & Cuccinello, H 2022, "Elon Musk says sleeping on factory floors was important so Tesla employees would 'give it their all,' days after a Twitter boss was pictured sleeping in the office", *Business Insider*, https://www.businessinsider.com/elon-musk-sleeping-habits-tesla-factory-floor-twitter-late-nights-2022-11, accessed 23 April 2024.

30 Garcia, A 2024, "11 Frugal Habits of Warren Buffett", *Yahoo! Finance*, https://finance.yahoo.com/news/11-ways-warren-buffett-lives-143051871.html, accessed 23 April 2024.

31 As Marx says, "[the capitalist's] own private consumption counts as a robbery committed against the accumulation of his capital". See *Capital: Volume I*, p. 739.

32 *Capital: Volume I*, p. 741.

33 *The Accursed Share: Volumes 2 & 3*, p. 199.

34 Solon, O 2016, "Under pressure, Silicon Valley workers turn to LSD microdosing", *WIRED*, https://www.wired.com/story/lsd-microdosing-drugs-silicon-valley/, accessed 23 April 2024.

35 Bataille, G 1985, "The Notion of Expenditure", in A Stoekl (ed.), *Visions of Excess: Selected Writings 1927-1939*, trans. A Stoekl, CR Lovitt & DM Leslie Jr, University of Minnesota Press, p. 117.

36 *Capital, Volume I*, p. 367.

37 Boltanski, L & Chiapello, È 2018, *The New Spirit of Capitalism*, trans. G Elliott, Verso, p. 152.

38 For its faults, the Justin Timberlake movie *In Time* understood this about its ham-fisted "time is money" analogy.

39 Ed Mylett 2019, "This is the GREATEST THING You Can Do Every Morning! | Ed Mylett", YouTube video, https://www.youtube.com/watch?v=dC67d0lzzAs, accessed 10 May 2024.

40 Evan Carmichael 2023, "You got 21 days a week", TikTok video, https://www.tiktok.com/@evancarmichael/video/7190531954926701830?lang=en, accessed 10 May 2024.

41 For more on this, see Takahahashi, M 2012, "Prioritizing sleep for healthy work schedules", *Journal of Physiological Anthropology*, vol. 31, no. 1, DOI: 10.1186/1880-6805-31-6. See also Costa-i-Font, J, Fleche, S & Pagan, R 2024, "Sleeping our way to being productive", *CEPR*, https://cepr.org/voxeu/columns/sleeping-our-way-being-productive, accessed 16 May 2024.

42 This is a short excerpt from Franklin's essay "Advice to a Young Tradesman", cited in *The Accursed Share: Volume I*, p. 126. Emphasis added.

43 Bataille, G 1991, *The Accursed Share: Volumes 2 & 3*, trans. R Hurley, Zone Books, p. 199.

44 Ibid., p. 198. See also *The Accursed Share: Volume I*, p. 190.

Sovereign Slackers: In Lieu of a Conclusion

1 The philosopher Jason Read has written extensively on negative solidarity, but for a freely available introduction, see Read, J 2019, "Negative Solidarity: The Affective Economy of Austerity", *Unemployed Negativity*, blog, http://www.unemployed-negativity.com/2019/10/negative-solidarity-affective-economy.html, accessed 12 August 2024.

STEAL AS MUCH AS YOU CAN

HOW TO WIN THE CULTURE WARS
IN AN AGE OF AUSTERITY

NATHALIE OLAH

Austerity has created suffering for millions, as well a generation beset with financial insecurity and crisis. Yet our TV, film, music, art and literature have never looked so rich, or so posh. During a period of immense struggle, the experiences of the majority have been pushed to the margins of our collective culture by the legacy media and its satellite industries – making it hard, if not impossible, to challenge those in power.

Steal as Much as You Can is the story of how this happened, exploring the rise of affluence in mainstream storytelling, and the corrosive effects of neoliberal and postmodern culture. By rejecting the established routines of achieving prosperity – and encouraging us to steal what we can from the establishment routes along the way – it offers hope to a bright and brilliant generation whose potential has suffered under these circumstances.

Order online from <u>RepeaterBooks.com</u>

REPEATER BOOKS

is dedicated to the creation of a new reality. The landscape of twenty-first-century arts and letters is faded and inert, riven by fashionable cynicism, ego-tistical self-reference and a nostalgia for the recent past. Repeater intends to add its voice to those movements that wish to enter history and assert control over its currents, gathering together scat-tered and isolated voices with those who have al-ready called for an escape from Capitalist Realism. Our desire is to publish in every sphere and genre, combining vigorous dissent and a pragmatic willing-ness to succeed where messianic abstraction and quiescent co-option have stalled: abstention is not an option: we are alive and we don't agree.